THE YEMENI WAR OF 1994
Causes and Consequences

The views expressed in this book are those of the authors alone. They do not necessarily reflect the views of the Emirates Center for Strategic Studies and Research.

© The Emirates Center for Strategic Studies and Research, 1995

British Library Cataloguing-in-Publication Data
A catalogue record for this book is available from the British Library

ISBN 0 86356 300 7 (hb)

The Emirates Center for Strategic Studies and Research
P.O.Box 4567
Abu Dhabi
United Arab Emirates

This edition first published in 1995
Saqi Books
26 Westbourne Grove
London W2 5RH

In-house editor: Jana Gough

The Emirates Center for Strategic Studies and Research

THE YEMENI WAR OF 1994
Causes and Consequences

Edited by Jamal S. al-Suwaidi

*Michael Hudson, Paul Dresch,
Charles Dunbar, Robert Burrowes
and Mark Katz*

Saqi Books

THE EMIRATES CENTER FOR STRATEGIC STUDIES AND RESEARCH

The Emirates Center for Strategic Studies and Research (ECSSR) in Abu Dhabi, United Arab Emirates, established March 14, 1994, is a research institution dedicated to carrying out independent scholarly investigations. As an independent center, the ECSSR plans to conduct scientific research and analyses of political, economic and social issues related to the UAE, the Gulf, and the Middle East regions. It seeks to provide a forum for the scholarly exchange of ideas on these subjects through the publication of books and research papers and the convening of conferences and symposia. The ECSSR also hopes to significantly contribute to the general educational and scientific development of the UAE.

The ECSSR is now in its second year of activity and will be significantly expanding its staff and programs to develop a major data base and information bank on Gulf topics; to be a source of up-to-date information through electronic means; to have a highly qualified research staff ready to conduct research projects serving specific and general needs; to conduct public lectures, seminars and training workshops; and to initiate contacts with comparable institutions worldwide and to engage with them in mutually beneficial professional endeavors.

Contents

Note on Transliteration	7
List of Abbreviations and Acronyms	8
Foreword	9
Introduction *Jamal S. al-Suwaidi*	11
Chapter One: Bipolarity, Rational Calculation and War in Yemen *Michael C. Hudson*	19
Conflict Between the 'Real Power Centers'	20
The View from the South	22
The View from the North	27
What About Democracy?	31
Chapter Two: The Tribal Factor in the Yemeni Crisis *Paul K. Dresch*	33
The Crisis	33
Which Tribes are Which	37
Tribalism as a System	42
Tribal Conferences	44
What is Tribalism?	54
Chapter Three: Internal Politics in Yemen: Recovery or Regression? *Charles F. Dunbar*	57
Five Scenarios	59
Conclusions	68

Contents

Chapter Four: The Yemeni Civil War of 1994: Impact on
   the Arab Gulf States
   Robert D. Burrowes   71
     Effects of the Civil War   71
     Undoing the Negative Effects   77
     Conclusion   79

Chapter Five External Powers and the Yemeni Civil War
   Mark N. Katz   81
     Siding with the South   82
     Siding with the North   85
     External Powers   86
     Future Implications and Choices   88

Conclusion
   Jamal S. al-Suwaidi   95

   Contributors   101

   Notes   103
   Select Bibliography   117
   Index   121

Note on Transliteration

The transliteration of Arabic in this volume is simplified but internally consistent. The *'ayn* ['] and significant *hamzas* ['] are shown but, in order to avoid encumbering the text with diacritical marks, the long vowels and emphatic consonants are not distinguished.

Proper names with widespread currency in Roman script are retained in their customary forms, e.g. Aden, Yemen, Riyadh, 'Ali 'Abdullah Salih.

Abbreviations and Acronyms

ECSSR   Emirates Center for Strategic Studies and Research
GCC   Gulf Cooperation Council
GPC   General People's Congress
NATO   North Atlantic Treaty Organization
PDRY   People's Democratic Republic of Yemen [South Yemen]
UAE   United Arab Emirates
UN   United Nations
US   United States
USSR   Union of Soviet Socialist Republics
YAR   Yemen Arab Republic [North Yemen]
YRG   Yemeni Reform Grouping (Islah)
YSP   Yemeni Socialist Party

Foreword

In response to the rapidly deteriorating situation in Yemen in 1994, which by May had resulted in open war, the Emirates Center for Strategic Studies and Research (ECSSR) convened a symposium on July 26–27, entitled 'The Yemeni War: Causes and Consequences' at which several area experts were invited to present their views.

Recognizing the importance of developments in Yemen and their consequences for regional security, and in accordance with the center's aim of promoting the scholarly exchange of ideas on topics relevant to the Gulf region, the ECSSR took this unique initiative even before a cease-fire had been declared.

The present volume contains the presentations given at the symposium. Through this publication, the ECCSR hopes to reach an international audience of institutions and individuals concerned with the Gulf region. The center believes that this work will make an important contribution to the literature of contemporary political development in the Arabian peninsula and promote a better understanding of the recent national conflict in one of its most strategically sensitive countries, Yemen.

Participating in the symposium were academics and practitioners from the Gulf region and abroad. Among those who presented papers were *Dr. Michael C. Hudson*, Seif Ghobash Professor of Arab Studies in the School of Foreign Service and professor of international relations and government at Georgetown University; *Dr. Paul K. Dresch*, lecturer in social anthropology at the University of Oxford and fellow of St. John's College; *Ambassador Charles F. Dunbar*, president of the Cleveland Council on World Affairs and former US ambassador to Yemen; *Dr. Mark N. Katz*, associate professor of government and politics at George Mason University and senior staff member at the George Mason University International Institute; and *Dr. Robert D. Burrowes*, research scholar at the Middle East Center, University of Washington in Seattle. I acted as moderator and discussant throughout the symposium.

Jamal S. al-Suwaidi
Director, ECSSR

Introduction

Jamal S. al-Suwaidi

Historians note that the existence of two civilizations in Yemen has been the norm. Whether dominated by a single outside power such as the Persians or the Ottomans, or on occasion dominated as a pair of virtually autonomous states by separate external powers, the Turks again in the north, and the British in the south, the people of Yemen have organized themselves as two societies. Relations between the two societies of Yemen have often been difficult, and consistently for at least the last century, the two Yemens have experienced a number of disputes. Open hostilities have occurred on several occasions, and unsurprisingly the two Yemens aligned with different major powers during the Cold War. Each Yemen also believes the other guilty of intrigue and manipulation, and indeed the assassination of Yemeni leaders of both societies has occurred. It is plausibly alleged that the leaders of the opposing Yemen sponsored these assassinations. More overt forms of the use of force have also been prominent. Throughout the 1960s and 1970s both Yemens engaged in revolutionary struggles, which ultimately subverted both the royal form of government in the north and the socialist form of government in the south. Typically, forces external to both Yemens, as well as forces from the opposing Yemens, participated in several of the bloody battles that precipitated government changes.

For the past decade, the leaders of the two Yemens have been experimenting with political integration, and predictably these tentative

Introduction

efforts have not yet produced significant change within the Yemen societies. Indeed, particularly in the case of South Yemen but also in North Yemen, albeit to a lesser degree, internal political integration is still very much an open question. Nevertheless, Yemeni leaders at least had begun the task of building a unified Yemen. Economic reasoning was prominent in the decision to seek reconciliation. South Yemen, during the Gorbachev years, increasingly realized less economic and military support from the Soviet Union. Both Yemeni leaders sought to reverse their economic misfortunes through exploitation of the newly discovered oil reserves at Shabwah.

On May 22, 1990, a long-standing Yemeni national dream became a reality when the Yemen Arab Republic (commonly referred to as North Yemen) and the People's Democratic Republic of Yemen (South Yemen) were united in the Republic of Yemen. The process of political integration was violently disrupted four years later, however, when certain historical legacies and divisive socio-political forces erupted, leading to civil war in 1994.

This book is an examination of the Yemeni civil war by area experts who presented their views at a symposium sponsored by the Emirates Center for Strategic Studies and Research and held in Abu Dhabi on July 26–27, 1994. Given the gravity of this event for Yemen and the political implications for the Arabian peninsula, the ECSSR assembled a number of distinguished scholars, researchers, and regional decision-makers to share their insights about a part of the world which for many is clouded in obscurity.

The causes and consequences of the conflict are discussed by Michael C. Hudson in his chapter, "Bipolarity, Rational Calculation and War in Yemen". Dr. Hudson focuses on the incongruity between the *de jure* and the *de facto* unification of North and South in 1990 and its impact on political and socio-economic integration. He points out that real unity is scarcely achieved by merging institutions, government authorities and legal codes without addressing lingering ideological and cultural differences among the governing élite. An appreciation of the role of these differences is important for an understanding of the collapse of the nascent national unity and the consequent civil war in 1994.

The events leading to the conflict are viewed from both the Northern and Southern perspectives. Light is shed on the behavior of the contending centers of 'real' power, emphasizing the lack of good faith

Introduction

in power-sharing arrangements and the mutual distrust that governed the relationship between North and South. Moreover, the influence of the Yemeni Reform Grouping (YRG or Islah) on the political maneuvering of the General People's Congress (GPC) and the Yemeni Socialist Party (YSP) is assessed, and the principal factors complicating a harmonious union are illuminated to explain attitudes of conspiracy and the eventual onset of periodic violence that preceded the full-scale conflict. The inherent tensions in wedding a socialist society with a traditional, tribal-dominated one are analyzed to discern, in particular, the extent to which the contending parties attempted to impose their view of the world on one another. Fear of Islamic extremism emanating from the North is contrasted with concerns of a Southern push to advance social progress at the expense of traditionalism. The chapter concludes with an assessment of the role of political participation in national unification and the ramifications of failure in its pursuit.

Tribalism in the contemporary political development of Yemen and its role in the recent Yemeni crisis is the focus of the chapter entitled "The Tribal Factor in the Yemeni Crisis" by Paul K. Dresch. An outline of tribal history in Yemen is followed by an assessment of tribalism's impact on the unfolding crisis, whether the 'tribal factor' entered precipitately or reactively, whether tribal allegiance carried over into political alignment among opposing forces, and how tribal identification impacted on the deteriorating climate between North and South. The opportunity for union is discussed in the context of the post-Cold War era, the collapse of the Soviet bloc, the dearth of foreign aid, and the ensuing economic malaise and rise in crime and violence in Yemen. How these events affected the relationship between the dominant tribes and the ruling élites is examined in order to illustrate the degree of tribal independence from central authority.

Viewed as increasingly distanced from this central authority, tribal affiliation may have been peripheral to the dynamics that shaped the political discourse at the top, but that must not cloud the fact that the very disposition taken by the tribal community entered the decision-making calculus of leaders on both sides. Indeed, the degree of isolation of the political leadership, which is believed to have given greater rein to a few individuals to eventually battle out their differences, stands in contrast to the community-based tribal efforts at resolving disputes through mediation. Hence, the discussion on tribal conferences provides a fresh insight into the debate over land disputes as well as relations

Introduction

with Saudi Arabia and political factions at home, such as Islah in the North and the socialists in the South. The asymmetrical influence exercised by tribal groupings in the North as opposed to the South is focused on to discern the effect on the sharing of political power. While tribalism may not completely capture the complexity of the Yemen crisis, it offers an instructive point of departure in examining how the political leadership, increasingly beholden to only a few, eventually became too detached from its 'natural constituency'.

The third chapter, "Internal Politics in Yemen: Recovery or Regression?", by Charles F. Dunbar, takes a broader look at the internal politics of Yemen to explain the victory by the San'a' regime and to present different interpretations of the civil war's outcome. To ascertain whether the North is likely to consolidate its power to ensure long-term rule, a measure of economic prosperity and balanced relations with competing political factions, the author lays out four alternative futures: the re-emergence of tribal power, a successful challenge from Islamic radicals, a reassertion of Southern secessionism, and national reconciliation and democratization. The conditions under which each scenario is likely to occur are contrasted with those that are believed to account for an enduring status quo with President 'Ali 'Abdullah Salih at the helm. The reasons for his continued leadership are examined in some detail, including his ability to restrict civil liberties without jeopardizing the loyalty of his constituency, to maintain a level of military spending while pushing for economic reform, and to pursue a measure of authoritarianism without encouraging unity among factions opposed to him.

Addressing the possibility of resurgent tribalism entails several issues of long-standing importance to Yemeni politics, including how far state authority has expanded at the expense of tribal influence over government policy. The chapter asks whether the state can co-opt the tribal leaders through an extension of commercial opportunities and examines the reasons why tribal leaders did not, in the end, constitute a viable threat to President Salih's power base in spite of readily available Saudi assistance. Similarly, the question is posed as to why the Islamic activists, and the YRG in particular, did not emerge as a more serious threat to Salih's rule, given the mounting challenge of religious groups elsewhere in the region (e.g. Saudi Arabia, Egypt, Algeria). Salih's ability to stem the radical influences of the religious and otherwise politically disaffected in the long run are also assessed.

Introduction

Finally, the chapter asks whether Southern political reassertion might again culminate in an attempt to secede, and analyzes the likelihood of a true democratization with meaningful political pluralism, considering Salih's leadership style and ideological predilections. These questions help synthesize the previous arguments and provide an opportunity to reassess Salih's ability both to invigorate the Yemeni economy and to keep political rivals at bay. They also help in understanding the significance of the 1994 civil war, and whether it was largely a peripheral event or a historic turning-point in Yemen's history.

Robert D. Burrowes' "The Yemeni Civil War of 1994: Impact on the Arab Gulf States" introduces a shift in focus away from the domestic context governing the crisis to the regional implications of the 1994 Yemeni civil war. In assessing the civil war's consequences for the Arabian peninsula as well as the reversibility of the negative fall-out, the author pays particular attention to Yemen's post-war capacity to influence events in the region, its relationship with Saudi Arabia and the functioning of a balance-of-power system in the area. The most populous country in the peninsula, a united Yemen merits special attention in its conduct with neighbors, its relationship with religious revivalist movements in the region, its handling of territorial disputes and its ability to hinder cooperation on regional issues. Saudi-Yemeni relations are examined in the wake of the 1990–91 Gulf war and the spillover of ensuing tensions into bilateral affairs during the civil war. Saudi Arabia's misgivings about its neighbor's proclivity to stray politically, to harbor irredentist feelings and to stir ideological sentiments are difficult to overlook. Hence, the analysis explores the chance for a future escalation of conflict between Saudi Arabia and a unified Yemen and how turbulence in their relationship affects the regional management of a balance-of-power system.

How such a system is largely confined to countervailing strategies involving domination, isolation and coalescing of countries in the peninsula is examined with reference to the seemingly incompatible needs for autonomy and internal as well as external security. The author's discussion of how Saudi Arabia's foreign policy is driven by domestic events provides a welcome insight at a time of mounting tensions with the country's Islamic revivalist faction. The potential for the other Arab Gulf states to act as an effective 'balancer' in response to shifts in the conduct between Yemen and Saudi Arabia is the key to understanding the long-term prospects for regional stability. In that regard, the stated proposals for reconciliation, accommodation and the construction of fluid alliances are instructive and may offer some reassurance to those seeking ways towards a truly peaceful coexistence in the Arabian peninsula.

The final chapter, "External Powers and the Yemeni Civil War" by Mark N. Katz, examines the implications for extra-regional powers and their reactions to the Yemeni civil war, and further expands on issues mentioned above that animate Yemen's relations with its peninsular neighbors. Fought outside the Cold War context and lacking the ideological element that used to separate East from West, the 1994 Yemeni civil war is examined from a decidedly different perspective, one that weighs the contribution of historically internal factors that surfaced in Yemen's previous civil wars against those factors that are of a discernibly external nature. The latter are analyzed in terms both of those countries that backed the South and of those that rallied behind the North. Given Saudi Arabia's cardinal role in the peninsula, Riyadh's position *vis-à-vis* the warring faction is detailed, most notably its call for an immediate cease-fire, and how its position differed from that of the other Gulf Cooperation Council states (GCC). Because lingering territorial disputes, the potential for large oil discoveries and the fear of spillover effects from attempts at democratization are all sources of instability for Yemen's internal condition as well as for its external affairs, it is difficult to isolate those effects that were limited to Yemen's foreign relations.

Suffice it to say that the motivations and actions of Yemen's neighbors in response to the 1994 civil war were inextricably linked to the 1990–91 Gulf war and the consensus among them to offer an 'Arab solution'. Although politically the Arab world mainly supported President Salih's regime in the North, each country took a nuanced response that was consonant with its unique set of interests. Katz examines whether this was also true for the West and how the Russian position—if indeed there was one—differed from that of its old nemesis. The North prevailed—but at what cost for the region and the world, and with how much outside help? The discussion seeks to answer those questions in an attempt to address the degree and character of possible future instability in Yemen and to ascertain the potential for radical states in the Middle east to manipulate Yemeni internal tensions. In this context, the issue of de-linking Saudi-Yemeni tensions from GCC politics is examined to determine whether countries such as Iraq and

Introduction

Iran could effectively play the 'Yemen card' to erode GCC unity. The author's view on how to defuse Saudi-Yemeni tension is a timely reminder of how difficult it is to bring about lasting peace in an area the world can ill afford to ignore.

Together, these writings offer a *tour d'horizon* of the principal issues that led to the 1994 conflict, that governed its outcome, and that are likely to resurface in some form should tensions in Yemen escalate again. Though by no means exhaustive, the views presented here are designed to deepen the understanding of scholars and laymen alike about a country and its people that will continue to influence in important ways the security and prosperity of the Arabian peninsula. Because of Yemen's defining role in the history of the region and its rather complex political evolution, recent events must not be subjected to parsimonious explanations. It is in that spirit that the following discourse hopes to inform the reader.

CHAPTER ONE

Bipolarity, Rational Calculation and War in Yemen

Michael C. Hudson

In trying to understand the causes of the 1994 civil war in Yemen, one is reminded of the distinction drawn by the French Middle East specialist, Pierre Rondot, in his analysis of Lebanon in the 1940s, between the *pays légal* and the *pays réel*.[1] One could attempt to explain Lebanon's politics in terms of its constitution and formal structures, but to get the full story one also had to focus on the actual centers of power in order to calculate the country's political behavior and stability. But we also need to look behind both the surface behavior of key actors and the institutional framework in which they (nominally at least) function to a deeper level of causation. We need to examine the factors that shape the behavior of institutions and the persons who wield real power. Does the structure and configuration of power in the domestic environment help explain why the 'players in the game' resort to violence to settle their differences?

In 1990, when Yemen embarked upon its historic experiment in unity and simultaneously its equally historic experience in democratization, many observers expressed optimism that both experiments would succeed.[2] Unified, pluralistic Yemen, it was thought, was developing a legitimate and stable political order. Most Yemenis were also optimistic: unity was a national dream that had eluded several efforts to achieve it over the past half-century and a liberal, multi-party, parliamentary system seemed a big advance over the authoritarian politics that had characterized, albeit in different ways, the two Yemeni states before unification. Unfortunately, by the spring of 1994 the visitor to San'a' found a country in which the democratic order was breaking down and the new-found national unity was being threatened. What was going wrong?

A full explanation of the *pays réel* would involve examining Yemen in terms of political culture, political economy and exogenous factors, among others. Such a comprehensive analysis is beyond the scope of this chapter. I shall concentrate instead on interpreting the origins of the Yemeni war in terms of the 'logic' of the conflict between competing 'real' centers of power. This approach is not so much concerned with determining who was responsible as with trying to understand the behavior of the contending parties as 'rational actors' competing in a high-stakes arena. To that end, I shall attempt to discover, or imagine, the logic of the situation as it appeared to the two main respective antagonists, Southern and Northern. This is not to suggest that the institutional level is less important: one should still ask how the various structures for governance and conflict resolution actually functioned or malfunctioned and whether the outbreak of war indicates fundamentally an institutional failure and, specifically, a failure of democracy.

Conflict Between the 'Real Power Centers'

In their 1957 path-breaking historical-comparative study of patterns of political integration, Karl Deutsch and his colleagues[3] proposed a useful four-cell matrix typology which examined different kinds of association between separate political communities in terms of two dimensions:

(i) whether they are amalgamated or non-amalgamated (whether or not there has been a formal merger of previously independent units); and

(ii) whether they are integrated or non-integrated (whether 'a sense of community and of institutions and practices' has developed to the point that dependable expectations of peaceful change are assured for 'a long time').

Despite the formal appearance of unity, the Yemens that were connected together in 1990 qualified as an 'amalgamated' system but not as an 'integrated' system—rather like the Hapsburg Austro-Hungarian empire before the First World War, but somewhat unlike the United States (an amalgamated, integrated security community) or Norway and Sweden (a non-amalgamated, but integrated pluralistic security community). While Yemeni unity (i.e. an amalgamation of the former independent Yemens) was achieved with a stroke of the pen on May 22, 1990, that historic day marked only the beginning of a process of political integration. The fact that the Yemenis, North and South, felt a sense of common identity on a cultural, historical and social level was in itself no guarantee that *political* integration could be taken for granted. And, in fact, beneath the surface of politics (the *pays légal*) the two political establishments that had been joined in the 'marriage' of unity, but not merged, were if anything maneuvering to maintain—and, indeed, to extend—their autonomy and power. On the formal level, the structures of an integrated polity were established—constitution, parliament, elections, bureaucratic 'mergers'. An arena for free political expression was opened—the press proliferated, parties and associations were established, conferences were convened. But on the level of the *pays réel*, the two former authoritarian power centers went into the merger lacking good faith and lacking trust in each other. While the General People's Congress (GPC) and the Yemeni Socialist Party (YSP) both agreed to a power-sharing formula, roughly on a 50–50 ratio, notwithstanding the 80–20 population disparity between North and South, these two establishments were also preparing fall-back strategies and contingency plans for expected conflict. Each side sought to build up its own military capabilities, paying only lip service to the principle of unifying the military. Each side cultivated external support. Both sides seemed to share a tacit interest in thwarting the development of independent political forces and in corrupting attempts by Yemen's emerging 'civil society' to enter into Yemeni politics in a serious way. Indeed, it was the emergence of a new player, the Yemeni Reform Grouping (YRG or Islah), that precipitated the open conflict between the GPC and the YSP.

It is impossible, so soon after the fighting, for outside observers to be fully cognizant of the detailed history of this rivalry and, consequently, to make an informed judgement as to which side was 'responsible' for the two-month civil war that left from 5,000 to 7,000 dead (government estimates were lower, opposition estimates much higher). But one can reconstruct the conditions leading to the conflict from Northern and Southern sources. While they obviously contradict each other, they do show persuasively how deeply each side distrusted the other. Mirror images of conspiracy created an 'objective' reality of their own. Whatever the truth, each side clearly suspected the worst of the other.

The View from the South

The YSP leaders who brought South Yemen into union with the North in 1990 appear to have done so in the belief that they would remain at least equal partners with the GPC regime in San'a'. At the same time, however, they harbored deep misgivings about what they saw as a closed, tribal-dominated Northern establishment. These are the perceptions that emerge from interviews with Southern politicians and from newspaper accounts. They suggest that the roots of the civil war extend back to the establishment of unity itself, three years before Vice-President 'Ali Salim al-Bid[4] began his self-imposed exile in Aden. Interviewed in June 1990, Prime Minister Haydar Abu Bakr al-'Attas contended that the two old systems, each of which had insisted on its respective exclusive approach to unity, had learned from recent Yemeni, regional and international experience. After the bloody upheaval in Aden in 1986, the YSP had come to see the virtues of unity and the drawback of partition. The YSP, and hopefully the GPC as well, had learned to compromise, 'and compromise is a new thing for Yemen'. Gone were the days of 'one party—one opinion'. But al-'Attas clearly had reservations about partnership with the regime in San'a' and he saw big problems ahead: backwardness, tribalism, sectarianism and socio-economic differences. He warned in particular of religious extremism. While stating that the YSP welcomed the Muslim Brotherhood in the new pluralist political order, he noted that the welcome depended on the Brotherhood's refraining from calling other parties (like the YSP) traitors or unbelievers (*kafirs*). The way to deal with these problems, he argued, was to extend the discipline (*nidham*) of the South to the anarchy (*fawda*) of the North. Without sound administration, there could be no end to the present corruption. One could infer from al-'Attas' remarks that he and his colleagues went into the unity as a calculated risk, expecting that they could eventually imprint *nidham* on their much larger partner, and thus achieve the progress and development that had always been the ideological core beliefs of the YSP.

Similar views were expressed by other left-wing politicians. Jarallah 'Umar, a YSP leader who had frequently been *persona non grata* in San'a', felt that times had changed and that both regimes had also changed. Previously, each party had wanted to destroy the other. Now there was more realism on both sides and it was possible 'to meet halfway'. But implicit in these comments is the assumption that each 'party' would remain a distinct player—unity thus did not mean the integration of these well-developed centers of power. And when asked if things could get worse again quickly, 'Umar replied, 'Yes, it is possible.' But he was ready to embark on this risky experiment of unity because democracy had become a more international phenomenon—including some states in the Arab world. On the other hand, he and a colleague worried that Saudi Arabia might try to undermine the unity experiment, not wanting to see a democratic system take root in the Arabian peninsula.

At the time of unification, the respected YSP leader Dr. Yasin Sa'id Nu'man noted that even before unification a pluralist tendency had begun to take root in the South, within the YSP, after the 1986 upheavals. As president of the new, transitional parliament (*majlis*), composed of the existing Northern and Southern legislatures, plus some thirty appointed representatives of other political tendencies, Dr. Nu'man argued that this parliament would have to play a central role if future political violence were to be avoided. With hindsight, we may observe that he was right. Unfortunately, the parliament, even after the first free nationwide elections in April 1993, failed to play a central role and violence in the form of civil war did occur. Despite his optimism, Dr. Nu'man was aware of possible dangers. He observed that the Northern political institutions were built upon traditional structures but that traditional structures had undermined social progress, thereby feeding instability. Speaking of the growing Islamist movement in the North, he asserted that, 'Our battle is on earth, not in heaven.' And, in a comment that speaks directly to the 1994 civil war, he observed that in the third world, 'The political will is stronger than the constitutional will.'

One may infer that the YSP and Southern leaders approached unification with mixed feelings. They knew how popular the ideal of Yemeni unity was for Yemenis, both North and South, and how politically advantageous it was to be associated with such a project. They had an agenda for 'development' that they hoped would submerge the tribalism, corruption and backwardness that they felt characterized Northern politics. They saw opportunities to join and eventually direct a greater Yemen whose socio-economic and political possibilities exceeded the decrepit conditions in the declining People's Democratic Republic of Yemen (PDRY). But they also feared that they might fall under the domination of a Northern political way of life for which they had no respect, and they were particularly concerned about the potential of the new but growing Islamist movement. In that unfortunate event, perhaps they also calculated that they could bail out of the unity experiment and restore—and dominate anew—an independent South Yemen. Throwing in their fortunes with 'Ali 'Abdullah Salih was a rational choice, a calculated risk, but for them it ultimately proved to be a mistake.

The YSP leaders soon realized that their calculations had gone awry. Saudi Arabia's reaction to Yemen's stand in the 1990–91 Iraq–Kuwait crisis dissipated the expected economic dividend of unity. The benefit of modest oil revenues was wiped out by the burden of the 800,000 Yemeni migrant workers forced to leave Saudi Arabia. Moreover, the Salih regime not only proved resistant to 'modernization' by Southerners, it also seemed bent on reducing YSP power by all possible means. Unity was less than a year old before Prime Minister al-'Attas had come to doubt the good faith of the Salih–GPC counterparts. The Northerners, he complained, from the beginning began moving more military-security and civil officials into the former South than had been authorized. 'The [Northern] Central Security Forces barracks in Aden', he observed sardonically, 'would serve 2,000 for lunch and 5,000 for dinner.' From the very beginning in 1990 and through 1993, according to al-'Attas, President Salih repeatedly flouted the power-sharing agreements under which unity had been achieved. He was particularly dismayed that his efforts at administrative reform and economic development, which culminated in a lengthy National Construction and Reform Programme (approved by the parliament in December 1991) was simply ignored by the president. Instead, al-'Attas asserts that Salih would make financial decisions on his own by going directly to the finance minister, bypassing the Council of Ministers as a body. Moreover, although there was a nominal 50–50 split of key positions between the YSP and the GPC, the YSP ministers found that the real decisions in their ministries were being taken by the GPC directors-general. There were not enough YSP or Southern civil servants at lower levels in the ministries in San'a' to prevent the more numerous Northern bureaucrats from dominating them.

Much the same situation prevailed in the military and security institutions. It had been agreed that there should be a substantial cut in the military establishment of unified Yemen, but it was impossible for the YSP minister of defence, Haytham Qasim Tahir, to implement either cutbacks or integration between Southern and Northern units. His decrees were simply ignored by the chief-of-staff, a Salih loyalist. Al-'Attas submitted a detailed 'terms of reference' document on military integration in April 1992, but action on it was postponed indefinitely. At the same time, the YSP leadership believed that the Northern armed forces were receiving military training from Iraqi officers brought to San'a' as 'teachers'.

More ominous still, from the YSP point of view, was a pattern of violence that began in 1991 and continued episodically right up to the outbreak of war in May 1994. More often than not, YSP officials and their relatives were the targets. Political and economic fall-out from the Gulf war led to what one Western journalist described as an 'unprecedented spate of violence' in September and October 1991,[5] and what al-'Attas depicted as the 'first crisis' of the unity period. The 'second crisis' unfolded during 1992. It consisted of a series of assassinations and intimidations of YSP officials, including the serious injuries inflicted on the YSP minister of justice, 'Abd al-Wasi al-Sallam, in the spring. Al-'Attas himself was the object of several attempts in 1992 and 1993, and his brother (a non-political man) was murdered in Aden in June. The house of Dr. Nu'man, the YSP parliament speaker, was hit by a rocket. When al-'Attas wrote to ask Salih to explain and deal with these incidents, the president blamed 'foreign elements' and did little else. Although the parliamentary elections finally held in April 1993 were judged by international observers to have been reasonably free, acts of intimidation continued, including the assassination of the dean of a teacher training school in Dhamar and, on October 29, the murder of Vice-President al-Bid's nephew. These events marked what al-'Attas calls the 'third crisis', and the prime minister finally departed San'a' in January 1994, fearing for his safety. The YSP accuses the San'a' security services, headed by the president's brother, of deliberately trying to intimidate and provoke the YSP into a secessionist position by such tactics.

In the light of all this, it seems reasonable to conclude that the YSP might have been convinced of the bad faith and aggressive intentions of President Salih and his entourage. Thus, when the National Dialogue Committee finally came up with its Document of Concern and Reconciliation (*wathiqat al-'ahd wa-l-ittifaq*), in which all of the sensitive issues were once again raised—security, administrative reform, decentralization, and so on—the YSP leadership may well have been extremely skeptical of the value of the president's signature on that document, perhaps to such an extent that it 'realistically' began to plan for secession and to mobilize regional support (mainly Saudi) for that purpose. Al-Bid's decision to fly directly to Riyadh and Kuwait after the signing of the *wathiqa* in Amman firmly convinced the San'a' establishment that the YSP had negotiated in bad faith and was now conspiring openly with its regional patrons to break Yemen apart.

The leadership of the breakaway 'Democratic Republic of Yemen' made its view perfectly clear in a *note verbale* it submitted to the UN Security Council special envoy, al-Akhdar al-Ibrahimi:

> As soon as the Gulf crisis erupted, the leadership of the former Yemen Arab Republic (YAR) breached all the unity agreements and worked through all means possible to enforce its own system upon the new nation . . . As soon as the government initiated these [the December 1991] reforms, the powerful members of the former Northern leadership—that opposed the unity, progress and modernization—waged an undeclared war against the leadership of the Yemeni Socialist Party. This was carried out by political assassinations and terrorism in many forms . . . Islamic fundamentalist forces were used in these terrorist attacks.

The *note verbale* goes on to accuse San'a' of initiating the series of military confrontations and Salih of making a speech on April 27, 1994 that were 'tantamount to a declaration of war'. Such is the justification for al-Bid's declaration of secession on May 21. Subsequently, the YSP accused seventeen San'a' officials, starting with 'Ali 'Abdullah Salih (and including several members of his family and tribe), of masterminding a conspiracy to drive the country to war.[6]

Bipolarity, Rational Calculation and War in Yemen

The View from the North

Conspiracy was also very much in the minds of the president and his entourage in San'a'. Northern officials claim that the plot to undo Yemeni unity was hatched in Geneva in 1992 at a meeting between a senior YSP leader and a high-ranking Saudi foreign-policy 'troubleshooter'. According to San'a''s interpretation, the conspiracy took concrete shape following the April 1993 parliamentary elections, in which the YSP had emerged in a diminished position. Yemeni government sources claim that as early as May 1993 the airline of former South Yemen, al-Yemda, had begun transporting light weapons from Lebanon and Egypt to Aden to bolster the YSP army. Beginning in October, arms shipments were detected being unloaded in Aden harbor. In January 1994 the plot, as Northern officials describe it, became fully operational. San'a''s intelligence services observed increasing amounts of military equipment arriving regularly in the former PDRY. Since the YSP itself presumably lacked the cash necessary to acquire MiG-29s, tanks, armored personnel carriers and other equipment from former Soviet bloc countries, San'a''s suspicions were directed towards Yemen's wealthy neighbors in the Gulf Cooperation Council (GCC).

The GPC-dominated government also discerned a pattern of subversion of the unified country's institutions by 'Ali Salim al-Bid and his supporters in the YSP. For example, when al-Bid was quoted in the Arab press in 1993 and in the run-up to the war in 1994 as questioning popular support for the floundering unity experiment, San'a' regarded such assertions as deliberately divisive. Then, in August 1993, al-Bid visited the United States for medical treatment, but he also arranged for a meeting in Washington with his American counterpart, Vice-President Al Gore. This move, taken without consultation with his colleagues on the Presidential Council, and outside the protocol channels of the Yemeni embassy in Washington, was interpreted in San'a' as another example of conspiratorial maneuvering—an attempt to enlist US support for the YSP cause. After this provocative maneuver, instead of returning to San'a' al-Bid went straight to Aden (he had done so the previous year for several months), refusing to return to the political capital and undertake his duties as a member of the Presidential Council. Several of his closest colleagues did likewise. President Salih's followers found this behavior nothing less than an effort to paralyze the government and ultimately wreck the unity.

Given these suspicions about YSP intentions, it is not surprising that the GPC also suspected a hidden agenda in the YSP demands for political reforms. Southern calls for administrative decentralization were seen as tantamount to separation. Southern complaints about San'a'-inspired assassinations of YSP officials were seen as gross exaggerations designed to promote separatism. Southern complaints about widespread corruption involving the president's inner circle of relatives were dismissed as groundless and designed to fan popular discontent. To Southern charges that the North was exploiting its resources, the Northerners countered that San'a' was basically underwriting the administration and development of a region that was virtually destitute after more than two decades of inefficient communist rule. Senior officials in President Salih's government rejected YSP charges that San'a' was dispatching civil servants (except for provincial governors) to the South to impose San'a''s will; on the contrary, they accused the YSP of expelling from Hadramawt many thousands of Northern casual laborers in 1993-94. Northern politicians argued that they had repeatedly 'walked the extra mile' in allowing Aden a far greater share of power in the unified government than its demographic weight would have justified. Not only had the Salih regime agreed to a 50-50 split in 1990, it continued to agree to disproportionate YSP representation even after the YSP's poor electoral showing in 1993. GPC spokesmen contended that their very participation in the extra-governmental National Dialogue Committee in autumn 1993 was a concession to YSP concerns and that they had accepted many of the YSP demands in drafting the *wathiqa*. In light of all this, the continuing boycott by many of the YSP leadership of government participation in San'a' came to be construed not simply as 'normal' political maneuvering but as a systematic campaign of subversion.

The Salih camp seems to have concluded at some point that there were more than mere policy differences with the YSP and that in reality the YSP was using these differences as a smokescreen to mask its real intentions. Those intentions, according to the president's men, were nothing less than to unseat Salih's 'ruling military family' (as the YSP called it) and/or to re-divide the country. The president was first and foremost a military man whose *métier* was security. After all, he had come to power under dangerous circumstances (his two predecessors had been assassinated) and had managed—to the surprise of almost everybody—to survive for some fifteen years in the rough-and-tumble of Yemeni politics, including war and insurrection. As one of his associates observed, he cannot but view the world through the lens of 'security'. While not as tyrannical, cruel or isolated as certain other Middle East leaders, one can imagine that by now he had acquired the habit of ruling with a firm hand. Moreover, having delegated several key military-security positions to his close relatives and tribal kinsmen, he had to be aware that there was an 'establishment' behind him that expected him to deliver the perquisites of power—and certainly not to allow others to infringe on them.

Of the several challenges facing the Salih–GPC establishment, three were perhaps crucial: the YSP, Islah and the economy. Certainly, the paramount threat was the YSP establishment, with its dominant, essentially 'sovereign' position in the South still largely intact. Above all, the fact that the YSP had the armed forces of the old PDRY at its disposal made this threat qualitatively different from the others. Scarcely less alarming was the support that it could apparently depend upon from certain neighboring countries. The logic of the situation (from both the GPC and YSP perspectives) was probably 'zero-sum': any gain for the YSP was a loss for the GPC, and vice versa.

The second challenge emanated from the growing Islamic reform movement represented in the Islah grouping. Some leaders of the Islamic tendency had originally opposed the idea of unity, fearing that the YSP—with its 'secular, communist' ways—would spread corruption were it to be allowed inside an enlarged Yemeni tent. Having been unable to prevent unity, which after all was very popular, Islah nevertheless continued to play a growing role as the major 'opposition' party to the ruling, power-sharing coalition of the GPC and YSP. As its popularity grew, so did its leverage against Salih and the GPC. Yemen's political logic, however, gradually drew the GPC and Islah closer together, and Islah's impressive showing in the April 1993 parliamentary elections must have revealed to the GPC the advantage of bringing it into the ruling coalition as a junior partner to reduce further the major threat posed by the YSP. Better still, Islah did not possess a professional army. Furthermore, the grouping's organizational porosity allowed the regime's security services to penetrate it. But Islah did have independent assets: a tribal base in the Hashid federation, headed by Shaykh 'Abdullah bin Husayn al-Ahmar, and a growing radical Islamist ideological appeal symbolized by Shaykh 'Abd al-Majid al-Zindani.

The Yemeni War of 1994: Causes and Consequences

President Salih's own tribe, Sanhan, was a part of Hashid. The president might well have calculated that if the YSP were to force on the GPC administrative reform and decentralization, and reform of the military-security apparatus, or (worse still) a breakup of the unity in which he had such a vital political investment, he might be ousted by an Islah/tribal faction from within his own entourage.

Thus, even though the GPC's loose alignment with Islah strengthened Salih by diminishing YSP relative power, it may also have restricted his freedom of maneuver. While the YSP was also alarmed by the challenge of a third party, especially one so ideologically hostile and inclined towards supporting its main adversary, the GPC, it nonetheless agreed to Islah's participation in government—perhaps anticipating that Islah might present a religious-conservative challenge to President Salih, and so increase YSP leverage with the president. But lacking an overall institutional framework of *nidham wa qanun* (law and order), unified Yemen could not contain the essentially destabilizing effects of transition from a bipolar to a tripolar power structure.

The third factor contributing to the Salih–GPC concern was the decline in Yemen's economy. The loss of an estimated $300 million annually in remittance income was a serious and continuing problem, as was the burden of nearly a million workers suddenly returned from Saudi Arabia. The serious economic riots in Ta'izz in December 1992 were a sign of latent discontent with the ruling authorities. Unemployment in 1993 was estimated at 36%.[7] The Yemeni riyal fell in value by 30% during the first year of unity and weakened still more as the crisis deepened after al-Bid's retreat to Aden in August 1993. The riyal, which was exchanged at 13 to the dollar at the time of unity was at 63 in February 1994 and had weakened further to 75 when the war broke out in May. Coming at a time of widely publicized significant new oil discoveries, ordinary Yemenis wondered aloud why their living conditions were declining and not rising. The newly liberalized press, especially in the North, gave vent to many of these complaints. The casual observer in San'a' during the months before the war began would frequently hear from middle-class Yemenis of various political persuasions (including the GPC) stories of corruption in high places. One could infer from all this that the Salih–GPC regime was no longer as popular or respected as it had been at the time of unification. A loss of prestige in future bargaining with the YSP, or worse still the loss of the South, might therefore have been viewed by the regime as further eroding its legitimacy and even, possibly, its stability.

Whether or not this situation was an inducement for the Salih regime to provoke a war in order to increase its popularity, as some Southerners have argued, is impossible to say. Assuming that President Salih was confident that he could win such a war, there is a certain logic to the argument. Logic, of course, is not a substitute for empirical evidence, so at this point it is premature to claim that San'a' deliberately intended to start the war. Indeed, Western military analysts in San'a' seemed convinced that the North's forces could not win a decisive victory, but they, along with the YSP leadership, turned out to have misjudged the situation.

What About Democracy?

As noted at the beginning of the chapter, any definitive conclusions about Yemeni unity and democracy must await a more comprehensive treatment than is possible at this time. Nevertheless, certain pertinent trends are evident. First, there was a powerful drive towards civil war because the 'logic of the situation,' as the two main antagonists probably perceived it, made it only 'rational' for them to behave in mutually threatening ways. The logic of the situation is far deeper and more significant than any alleged personal antagonism between the 'two 'Alis'. It involves two ruling establishments, each complex and organized, and each with capabilities, intentions and interests. The rational interests and *power* of these two establishments also override the 'ideological glue' of unity as a widely held popular value. There is no reason to believe that unity is not widely and deeply valued by ordinary people, but that clearly is not sufficient to maintain the integration of formerly independent entities.

Second, it seems clear that the liberal, multi-party electoral and parliamentary institutional matrix, so carefully constructed to manage conflict, nurture the newborn unity and promote good government, was unable to override the logic driving the two power centers towards war. It was fascinating, if ultimately disappointing, to observe how Yemenis right across the political spectrum—from tribal leaders to secular intellectuals—strove to mobilize 'the general will' against the destructive logic of the Northern and Southern 'commands'. As Sheila Carapico has demonstrated in several papers, the 1990–94 period was marked by an efflorescence of 'public activity' and 'civil society'.[8] There were conferences, policy debates and peaceful demonstrations urging the power-holders to abjure violence and preserve unity. The fact that war finally broke out should not obscure the point that Yemeni society was making important progress towards orderly, participatory politics. Even though the GPC and YSP leaderships were ultimately driven by the rational calculations of antagonists in an anarchic environment, both had moved significantly towards accepting a liberal order, compared to their pre-unity behavior.

In 1990 a conjuncture of historical circumstances had finally made Yemeni unity possible. The act of unification required, for the most pragmatic reasons, political liberalization. In theory, the newly established unity would henceforward be maintained and deepened through the *nidham wa qanun* of multi-party, liberal, constitutional politics. To conclude that democracy was an inadequate means for preserving the unity assumes that the unity itself had actually been achieved. Yet we know that 'unified' Yemen was not 'integrated' in Deutsch's terms. To expect liberal democratic institutions to preserve—or indeed, create—integration in a polity that was still divided into two *de facto* sovereign power centers—the *pays réel*—is perhaps expecting too much. Some Middle Eastern leaders and commentators have criticized San'a', asserting that unity cannot be created by force. But that assertion is not historically supportable, certainly not to any student of American history. Costly as it has been, the 1994 Yemeni civil war may have paved the way for real unity through the elimination of a rival 'sovereignty'. It remains to be seen: (a) whether the war has in fact led to this result; and (b) if so, whether the rulers of this more integrated Yemen will move down a liberal democratic path (as they have pledged to do) or whether they will revert to their past authoritarian ways. If the lesson they draw from the civil war is that Yemen is not 'ready' for democracy, they may give in to their dictatorial instincts. That would be the wrong road to take, and a costly one. The imprisonment and beating of journalists in San'a' in July 1994 was not a good sign, and one must hope that it was an isolated example of post-war excess. In a Yemen that has only one locus of sovereignty but which is a complex, diverse and pluralist society, the truer lesson of the war is that political participation and pluralism is the only way to build genuinely legitimate—and stable—government.

CHAPTER TWO

The Tribal Factor in the Yemeni Crisis

Paul K. Dresch

Political scientists in the present volume deal largely with the actions of states. The anthropologist (in some ways, the odd man out) is asked to cover tribes and in doing so risks disappointing a political audience.[1] Put briefly, there was no tribal factor in the 1994 Yemeni crisis: that fact is itself significant. The Western press and Arabic press alike dwelled on which politician belonged to which tribe. Yet none of the major tribes joined in the fighting as a tribe. Indeed, to call this a civil war was to stretch a point—to call it an extended *coup d'état* would be as accurate.[2]

This chapter will begin with a brief sketch of structural factors before the crisis. The place of different tribes and of tribalism in Yemen's recent history will be outlined in two short sections. The major tribal conferences and organizations that flourished after Yemeni unity in 1990 will then be reviewed. We should then be in a position to assess not only what limits tribalism places on the country's politics, but also what opportunities it offers to those concerned to see Yemen prosper.

The Crisis

The 1990 union proceeded from South Yemen's bankruptcy. With the collapse of the Eastern bloc, there was nowhere to turn—and the pattern of oil exploration, which later pulled Vice-President 'Ali Salim al-Bid's people towards secession, at that time pulled the leadership in Aden towards the best deal they could get.³ The North seemed to take in the South, as West Germany some months later took in East Germany. The balance of the two erstwhile governments, latterly in the form of the General People's Congress (GPC) (*al-mu'tamar al-sha'bi al-'am*) and the Yemeni Socialist Party (YSP) (*al-hizb al-ishtiraki al-yamani*), encouraged a large measure of pluralism; a plethora of minor parties flourished, speech became as free in the towns as it had always been in the Northern countryside, the press became genuinely open, and parliamentary debates broadcast on Yemeni television were of a standard and interest matched only by occasional committees in the United States Congress.

Only a doctrinaire reading of history could discount the importance of what happened.⁴ But the parties brought with them their different pasts. The GPC was established in the North, at the start of the 1980s, as an alternative to party politics. Local committees were supposed to elect regional committees, the whole culminating in a national committee structure through which the will of the people would be known to those ruling. This was received with enthusiasm. Very rapidly, however, the system came to work in the opposite direction to that advertised, drawing little to the center except taxes and commanding the periphery, top-down, through an elaborate system of patronage. The state became a family business. Around the family there developed what I have elsewhere called a military-commercial complex.⁵ On a stack of bank-notes in 1990, someone had written (rather beautifully in felt-tip pen so it looked at first glance as if it was printed) on note after note in what must have been hours of compulsive anger, 'Yemen, the land of a million colonels'. High-ranking army officers and a few great merchant families all had their hands in each other's pockets. Between them they had the state in their control.

A certain impatience with what was happening was expressed even at tribal weddings:

O Capital, Sayyah's a place of good reputation.
[What you've done] is a grudge against good and not acceptable.
If Sanhan, for instance, ruled paradise a year,
They'd write on the door, 'No Khawlanis'.

Such complaints were on the whole good-natured. They point,

however, to a genuine problem in so far as a family-based system of rule has become deeply entrenched during the last ten years. The president, one might guess, no longer has the freedom of action he had at the start of the 1980s.[6] (In what follows I shall therefore use the neutral phrase 'the president's men'; to blame the president personally, as his opponents do, is not wholly realistic.)

After unity in 1990, many groupings, not least among the Northern tribes, saw the chance that things might be ordered differently. But this was not a crisis. A good deal of money remained in private hands. The government's budget remained a work of imagination (if the government came up short, as it usually did, neighboring states could be relied on to shift a hundred million dollars or so to the Central Bank). With the 1990-91 Gulf war, the situation changed: some 800,000 Yemenis were forcibly repatriated, with the inevitable surge in immediately available cash and the prospect thereafter of bankruptcy. Hand-outs from Yemen's neighbors would now come only at a very high price politically. The upheaval of 1990-91 accentuated, although it did not cause, structural problems which turn upon the centralization of wealth and power.

In the Northern countryside (known as *bilad al-qaba'il*, the land of the tribes) around 1990, one saw several occurrences which had formerly been rare. The most noticeable of these was theft and banditry. There had always been problems within tribes and between them, but the theft of cars, for instance, had earlier been supposedly in response to a previous affront, a matter for public claims and rhetoric within forms of conflict and resolution understood by everyone. Now there were instances of random violence.[7] There were increasing reports of 'gangs' of thieves, and attempts by the tribes to contain these often led back to connections with the government apparatus. The same was happening among those whom the newspapers called the 'business community'. Deals were thwarted, business was blocked and everything was seen as depending upon a very few men in power. As the economy stalled so the tribes in the countryside, who had once been the basis of urban power, were increasingly distanced from the state. The dominant theme in tribal affairs, between 1990 and 1994, was self-preservation.

Throughout the period neither of the two regionally based parties, the GPC and the YSP, proved willing to attempt public politics. There were ample occasions, not least during 'Ali Salim al-Bid's later absences in the South, when President 'Ali 'Abdullah Salih might have

The Yemeni War of 1994: Causes and Consequences

maneuvered him towards the periphery by public openness—and there were obvious divisions in the YSP to play on. In his earlier spells in the South, al-Bid himself might have made public the issues he held against President Salih.[8] Both preferred a more private style. An important point was passed when the two 'Alis met at Hudaydah in late 1992. Until then al-Bid and the YSP had been de facto heads of the opposition, a category which included the smaller urban-based parties, the more interesting of the Islamic (though scarcely 'Islamist') parties and sundry tribal organizations based predominantly, although not exclusively, in Bakil. The Hudaydah meeting produced the usual expressions of eternal brotherhood. But what was said between the two 'Alis remained a mystery even to those of rank and influence.[9] The broad movement of opposition, which had centered for a while around al-Bid, henceforward kept its distance. Part of the reason that so little was seen of tribes in the fighting is that none of them, from late 1992 onwards, really trusted either side.

In retrospect, the Northern leadership's decision to fight may have been taken as early as February 1994. But it still seemed unwise to have a war. It was not necessary to be Erwin Rommel in order to see that the North could not defeat the South in short order (not short enough to preempt efforts at mediation), and the political cost of a long campaign might be high. Northern units trounced Southern units at 'Amran and Dhamar. The South, doubtless feeling the noose was closing, lashed out at San'a'.[10] A Southern government duly emerged, containing not only YSP men but, for instance, 'Abd al-Rahman al-Jifri (the constituents of the Southern government were unimaginable in circumstances apart from war). In the North, virulent speeches were heard not only from the military but from technocrats from whom something more restrained might have been expected.[11] In retrospect, therefore, everything seemed inevitable—a matter of North versus South. It was not.

The cynic might dismiss tribal conferences and peace demonstrations in the cities as unrealistic. The game of nations, they will claim, is played elsewhere. But several Yemeni politicians of sufficient weight to impress the most dedicated enthusiast of a 'great man' view of history worked hard to avert the fighting—the list of members of the National Dialogue Committee contains famous as well as interesting names. With tribes in mind, let us mention two: Sinan Abu Lahum of Nihm (Bakil), something of an elder statesman in Yemeni politics, and Mujahid Abu

Shawarib of Kharif (Hashid), a man almost unique for the respect he commanded from Northerners and Southerners alike. Both left Yemen with harsh words: not for some intractable problem between North and South, not for tribal conflict, nor even for the old favorite of 'foreign interference', but for differences among a small group of politicians.[12]

It is not for a foreigner to judge the truth of claims and counter-claims. In any case, history moves on. Those involved will wish to build relations anew. But the character of the 1994 crisis did derive in part from the isolation of the political leadership (or leaderships) from other parts of society, not least from the tribal system.

Which Tribes are Which

There are three large groupings of tribes in North Yemen—Hashid, Bakil and Madhhij. In South Yemen there are tribes which potentially attach to the last of these (al-'Awadhil could make this claim if they wished), there are tribes which attach to separate groupings from Shabwah out to Oman, and there are tribes which stand in splendid isolation, most notably Yafi'—'the Hashid of the South', as some Northerners called them. The place of these tribes in national self-presentation differed between the two Yemens.[13]

The South for years condemned *'asha'iriyyah* (tribalism) and identified this with *iqta'iyyah* (feudalism). Ethnographically that is simply wrong. Those areas that are, or were, in any way feudal are not very tribal. The tribal areas are not feudal. What sense the equation made derived solely from the modernist assumption that both are 'backward'.[14] The results of such rhetoric were appalling: village headmen, who owned no more than anyone else, were murdered by the state as 'feudal landlords', and in later years a person was as likely to be 'disappeared' for tribalism as for other sins. The 'new YSP' after unity was willing to use Northern tribes in practice, but no more ready than of old to accept tribalism at the level of political theory. In the South it cultivated alarm about re-tribalization. Tribes met again, certainly. They did nothing alarming. The return of erstwhile rulers (the 'feudalists,' some of whom by now were also extreme Islamists) was certain to worry the YSP, but the tribes of these areas acted primarily to mediate the disputes of others and, as with the Northern tribes (though in a different setting), to preserve themselves from dangers produced by non-tribal politics.[15]

In the course of the fighting, so far as can be gathered, Southern tribal areas wisely did little. The 'Awlaqis seem simply to have let the Northern army through, protesting that the battle was not their concern; so did the tribes of Radfan, as few in numbers and as conspicuous on the map as they were in colonial times. People from Yafi' went home in large numbers and simply stayed there. Attempts by al-Bid to rally 'the tribes of Hadramawt' produced no response.[16] What else could have been expected?

The North was more accepting of tribal identity. But here the constancy of language obscures shifts in social structure. Changes in the North during the 1980s teased tribalism apart into two rather different things: *mahsubiyyah* (a set of patronage relations), which ties the holders of power to dependants in Yemen and to sponsors abroad; and *qabaliyyah* or *qabyalah* (tribalism) as most tribespeople came to understand it, which is more a code of manners—or perhaps of procedure—that depends on the pretence of moral equality. The drawing apart of two aspects which had once coexisted easily was marked by the prominence of a single word: *taba'ud*, the 'distancing' of major shaykhs from their followers. The complement was that tribalism (*qabyalah, a'raf al-qaba'il, al-'adat al-qabaliyyah*) became objectified, no longer being the common sense of how things are but an ideology prescribing how things ideally should be. Journalistic, and sometimes diplomatic, coverage tends to ignore such distinctions. The assumption is often made that tribes are solid blocs that act as such, which is seldom true. To talk in terms of tribe against tribe—of simple aims and alliances—is usually misleading: the game of nations provides a poor model for the ways in which tribesmen act.

The government, some would argue, 'extended its control into tribal strongholds'. This is true in so far as there were more soldiers around and people registered their motor-vehicles; but such imagery suggests that tribes and government were separate entities, which initially they were not. Tribesmen held government jobs. Tribal leaders were prominent in the state apparatus and also in trade—where they were not 'co-opted', but from an early date were actors in their own right.[17] It is not so much that state control spread across North Yemen like an oil-slick. Rather, a small class emerged (some of tribal background, some not) whose interests became distinct from those of their immediate neighbors. The distinction between those in power (the state, roughly speaking) and society at large arose within a previously quite integrated setting. The extreme case (indeed, a unique case) is 'Abdullah bin Husayn al-Ahmar, the paramount shaykh (*shaykh mashayikh*) of Hashid.

Shaykh 'Abdullah has been at the center of Yemeni affairs for thirty years, a man of vast experience. But his position has looked increasingly problematic. Long before 1990 it was said that proposals had been made in Saudi Arabia to remove 'Ali 'Abdullah Salih and that Shaykh 'Abdullah had firmly rejected these (some might say on 'tribal' grounds). In the crisis of 1994 he stood by the president just as firmly—to the point, indeed, where many people spoke of him as the master-mind of Northern politics. Whereas relations between San'a' and Riyadh are one thing, those between Al Saud and Bayt al-Ahmar are quite another. It might be thought, however, that an alliance between Saudi Arabia's oldest (doubtless closest) contact in North Yemen and the man in Yemen (perhaps in the whole peninsula) whom the Saudis like least is an alliance with severe limitations.[18] 'Tribalism' seems a weak description of the complex relations being managed here.

With encouragement from friends in Saudi Arabia, Shaykh 'Abdullah co-founded the Yemeni Reform Grouping (YRG or Islah). Although the grouping is sometimes spoken of as a 'fundamentalist' party, it is actually a party that contains fundamentalists—a rather different thing.[19] Briefly put, tribesmen involved with Islah generally dislike the fundamentalists and the fundamentalists dislike the tribesmen; disagreement over how the state should be run divides the same two groups at the party's highest levels; and the more extreme of the fundamentalists at best overlap Islah's boundaries—those within Islah could go their own way if policy does not suit them and join those already outside, some of whom oppose Islah fiercely.[20] In short, here is another set of alliances that lacks much basis for solidity. The idea of Shaykh 'Abdullah leading a state of 'Arab Afghans' is not plausible. The divisions within Islah, which seem belatedly to have caught Saudi press attention,[21] have nothing whatsoever to do with tribes.

Finally, Shaykh 'Abdullah assumed the post of speaker of Yemen's parliament. This was not a post that suited his particular style and skills, but more importantly it completed the process by which he came to be identified by others (not least by men in Hashid) as a man of parties and of government. The people who were closest to him in the 'tribal' scheme found the change most difficult. Between 1990 and 1994 there was, within Hashid, a veritable explosion of stories blaming the Shaykh for his men's misfortunes. Most of these stories probably had little basis. What matters, however, is that people assumed that involvement with the country's rulers was somehow at odds with the role of a tribal shaykh.

With a firm tribal base, it might be possible to stand in the midst of conflicting tendencies and simply bend them to a single purpose, but that is not what the Shaykh was doing—and one doubts that in the 1990s anyone could do it, for tribalism is now riddled with contradictions. Shaykh 'Abdullah used to be referred to as *shaykh mashayikh al-yaman* (paramount shaykh of Yemen). That is not a phrase that is heard any more. A decade ago, within that form of common knowledge, Hashidis used to boast that their tribes, unlike others, were united 'like an army unit'. That is not a boast I have heard from a Hashid tribesman for a long time: indeed many of them seem demoralized. Although it is hard to imagine tribes ever acting against the Shaykh—he is held in great respect, and rightly—it is just as hard to imagine tribes (Hashid included) acting with him in the way they used to even twenty years ago. The Shaykh's undoubted influence has little to do with traditional *'asabiyyah* (solidarity based on tribe).

Appearances are deceptive. The newspaper *al-Watan al-'arabi*, for reasons of its own, envisaged a 'scenario' in which 'Ali 'Abdullah Salih was removed from power and replaced as president by the Shaykh, at the urging of high-ranking Hashid officers, 'by virtue of his tribal leadership' (*bi-hukmi zi'amati-hi al-qabaliyyah*).[22] Turn where one will, runs this kind of argument, there is only Hashid. The claim is sometimes replicated by tribesmen, but usually, it must be admitted, when they get things dramatically wrong:.

> Sanhan's part of Hashid, and Hashid's 'Abdullah's servant.
> Whatever the Saudis say, 'Abdullah says, fine with me.
> Serjeant 'Ali's become servant of the Haram's servant.
> The White House watches over all, controlling everything.

What President Salih or King Fahd would make of this is impossible to say (Shaykh 'Abdullah would surely find it laughable) and the US State Department might only wish it were so. The poem presents a wonderfully paranoid muddle. In the more informed tribal circles, whether Hashidi or Bakili, one no longer hears people speak like this.

In so far as Hashid did come to run the state at the end of a previous civil war (circa 1970), most Hashidis were as alienated from the holders of power as most Bakilis or people from Madhhij. Shaykh 'Abdullah himself is from al-'Usaymat. It would be hard to think of a particular tribe that benefited less from the Republic's victory. The only explicit opposition within al-'Usaymat centered around the Hashid Solidarity Conference, which is not large; but in the purely hypothetical case of voting for parties in 1992–93 and not for named candidates, more than half of al-'Usaymat might well have voted YSP. Certain other tribes of Hashid (Kharif and Bani Suraym) have done better, securing jobs in the army and the civil service. Yet even they encounter a 'glass ceiling', for the real power lies with only two tribes, Hamdan San'a' and Sanhan. The second is the president's tribe.

Sour references by tribal notables to *al-usrat al-malikah* (the royal family) or *al-usrat al-hakimah* (the ruling family)[23] are understandable when one considers how tightly knit are the military connections. President Salih's brother Muhammad commands Central Security, his half-brother 'Ali Salih 'Abdullah is in charge of the Republican Guard,[24] Muhammad Salih runs the air force, 'Ali Muhsin Salih the First Armored Division, and so on. Sundry other Sanhanis have been promoted beyond their abilities, and sundry Hamdanis with them. The First Armored Brigade, which were part of the initial fighting at 'Amran, had a Hamdani commander who was reduced to loafing at home and chewing *qat* because of the presence of a Sanhani chief-of-staff. Undue promotions of Sanhanis and Hamdanis were one cause of an attempted coup as early as 1979 (Dhu Muhammad were heavily implicated). Thereafter the state apparatus was better able to preempt such moves, but it was no longer popular. Nor can one speak of Hashidi dominance when the benefits of power are confined to such a small circle.

Hamdan and Sanhan are effectively suburbs of the capital, San'a'. Historically they were marginal to tribal affairs, being usually under the control of some city-based imam or some pretender to the throne. Now they have the throne. Ahmad al-Ghashmi of Hamdan and 'Ali 'Abdullah Salih of Sanhan worked against Ibrahim al-Hamdi, whose own intention, as Hashidis read it, seemed to be to replace an existing officer corps with men from these two small tribes. Presumably the attachment of Hamdan and Sanhan to the city was more compelling than the suggestion that both were in some sense Hashidi. The attachment to centralized patronage, on which al-Hamdi based a fatal miscalculation, has become far stronger—Hamdan and Sanhan are indeed now part of the city-world and belong to the tribal system only nominally.

When al-Ghashmi came to power, men from Hashid thought at last they might be back in favor. But the rise of President Salih was never conceived in particularly 'tribal' terms: from the outset the issue was the army, recruitment to which may certainly show a tribal bias but the structure of which is not tribal. From a tribal perspective, Sanhan are effectively newcomers; nor did any stories gain wide currency that might give them a grander past. It should be noted in passing that some in the South made play with the phrase, 'the Bayt al-Ahmar gang'.[25] In fact the name of President Salih's village simply happens to be the same as that of Hashid's leading family; there is no tie of shared descent. What practical links there are tend to be spoken of by tribespeople in terms not of *qabaliyyah* (tribalism) but of *mahsubiyyah* (patronage). The term *qabaliyyah* is used more by intellectuals who are not themselves part of the tribal system.[26]

Tribalism as a System

Tribesfolk are subject to the same economic and political pressures as other people. They do, however, have recourse to other means of response: not rioting (as the urban poor might) or withdrawing one's capital (as can business people), but appealing to certain forms of refuge and the settlement of disputes. When tribalism dominated the North, this set genuine limits as to what was likely. Even the long civil war of the 1960s was not the massacre it otherwise might have been (save of course for the Egyptian army). In the 1970s, caught between two opposed states (and interfered with at times by more states besides), North Yemen survived well enough: if the tribes could be set against each other, they also made certain that nothing too destructive happened by containing disputes in their own ways.

These ways included two essential principles of tribal custom. First, refugees from other tribes who found themselves at odds with their neighbors should always be taken in. ('Political allegiance notwithstanding, we took in them and they took in us until a settlement was reached with our fellows.') Tribalism thus acted as a buffer, absorbing and dissipating the shocks thrown at it. Second, arbitration between tribes who were in dispute could be undertaken by anyone of standing, not only by someone related to the disputing parties. The result was that neither the extent of the influence of the shaykhs nor the course of events could be read in a simple way from the tribal map. Political alignments were untidy. Those tribes that were predominantly royalist in the 1960s were predominantly socialist in the 1970s, and it is certainly untrue to say that 'the tribes' as a whole viewed the South before unity as 'atheistic and alien': some did, but others thought the South quite splendid.[27] More important, however, opinions can be broken down within tribes. To say, for instance, that 'Iyal Yazid are Nasiris is like saying that Michigan is Democrat—it would have to be subject to a great deal more qualification.

Not all the Northern tribes were anti-South, any more than all of Hashid had been republican, or all of Bakil royalist, thirty years before. Some tribes were very patient with the Saudis (indeed, there were probably few people anywhere who were real enthusiasts) whereas others, despite the money, were generally anti-Saudi. What concerns us here is the way in which tribalism in recent years has peeled away from the conduct of state power. Let me give two examples.

'Abdullah Daris, although he continued working with the president thereafter, resigned as governor of Ma'rib after finding that the local military commander (a senior officer from Sanhan) was receiving orders from San'a' behind his back. Bayt Daris are famous shaykhs of Dhu Muhammad. The initial problem concerned little more than vehicle registration. By the time that troops had finished throwing their weight about (ill-advised conduct with tribesmen on grounds of sense as well as manners), the area from Ma'rib to the Upper Jawf had become almost a war-zone. The garrison at al-Hazm was intermittently under siege. Such disorders reached not only eastward towards the desert but westward into Nihm, where as early as 1989 soldiers had hauled a woman of good family from a truck and supposedly broken her arm. That 'Abdullah Daris resigned is understandable. None of these problems was a matter of tribe against tribe, but of tribalism (a code of manners as much as anything) being flouted by state functionaries.

Events in the Jawf provoked an outburst that briefly acquired folkloric status when Mujahid Abu Shawarib (of Hashid, if it matters) reportedly shouted down the phone at the president that 'striking the heads of the Yemeni tribes' in this way—any of the Yemeni tribes— meant striking all of them. This was not a 'political' statement. Again, a code of manners or procedure was at issue. These worries about state conduct in San'a' reflected more immediate worries in the countryside, where people were genuinely at risk.

'Ali Hasan bin Jallal and Muhsin 'Ali bin Mu'ayli of 'Abidah were invited to help settle the problem between Nihm and the soldiers. Luckily for them, they were talking in a worn-out truck at the tail of the convoy when it was stopped at an army check-point and sprayed with bazooka and small-arms fire. The tribes claimed, whether rightly or wrongly, that the mediators had been set up by the local commander of troops (again an officer from Sanhan). When one asks why anyone would do this, one is referred to the mediators' role in solving troubles on the 'Abidah–Murad front—peace-making had become a dangerous business. The general assumption among shaykhs of different tribes is that the government (they include in this certain more influential shaykhs) is out to divide and rule. The accusations lead back to dubious land-deals whose scale seems scarcely commensurate with the trouble caused.

Lest it seem that the GPC was the only group in this position, let us mention al-Hada, 'Ans and the tribes south of San'a'. A plot of land was at issue in Haddah, a suburb of San'a' where the *nouveaux riches* have built villas in doubtful taste. Quite what happened will never be known, but in 1992 a tribal claimant to this land was shot dead by soldiers whose connections supposedly reached back this time to Salim Salih of the YSP.[28] Mediation was attempted at government urging. Al-Hada and 'Ans rejected it. A later attempt succeeded in containing the dispute, precisely because the shaykhs in this later attempt were not the government's men. The one point at which al-Hada's claims coincide with the military-commercial complex is that they rejected mediation by people linked closely with wealth and power. Their rejection was not of a specific party but of anyone in the then ruling coalition. Ten years earlier, people would have been delighted to secure mediation from a shaykh with government connections (which great grouping of tribes he belonged to was irrelevant). Now it was better to exclude such people.

Tribal Conferences

Conferences convened by tribes, and in tribal terms, have been a feature of North Yemeni politics since early in the civil war—since the 1963 'Amran Conference, in fact. The 1965 Khamir Conference is well known. In 1974 there was a major attempt by Shaykh 'Abdullah, when he and Ibrahim al-Hamdi were still on good terms, to form a tribal conference for all Yemen. After al-Hamdi's time there were several large meetings of Bakil. Part of this has been written on elsewhere, but the explicit aim was to restore Bakil to what Bakilis thought its rightful place.[29] Although the Yemeni press, as much as the foreigners, kept writing of Bakil as a bloc contesting the spoils of state, by 1992 or so this style had been dropped by the more interesting Bakil leaders. The reappearance of a Bakil Council has a slightly dated ring.[30] Nevertheless Bakil and Hashid seem the terms that journalists and governments expect.

One of the more intriguing features of the late 1980s and early 1990s was the reappearance of Madhhij, most of whose constituent tribes had previously been speaking of themselves as part of Bakil; the claim to be part of Hashid's opposite doubtless made more sense than being simply tangential to affairs of state. A brief account of how the revival started will give the flavor. Trouble among Murad, Khawlan al-Tiyal (definitely a Bakil tribe), al-Qayifah, al-Hada and Anis (sometimes a Bakil tribe, by its members' estimate, sometimes Madhhij) had persisted for years, as it had between Murad and 'Abidah and among the tribes of the Jawf. The feeling grew (first, probably, on the 'Abidah front) that these troubles were exacerbated by the state.[31] A meeting of several Madhhij shaykhs was held in Saudi Arabia. By most accounts, Ghalib al-Ajda' was the favored candidate to be paramount shaykh, but opposition from within his own tribe denied him a formal *tahjir*.[32] On his return, again by most accounts, he was dissuaded by the president from pursuing the matter. A year or so later Nasir al-Dhahab of al-Qayifah was murdered, people assumed because of his efforts to resolve tribal differences.

Nonetheless, the shaykhs of the various Madhhij tribes had been thrown together. Increasingly they began to meet and to assess their problems. With unity they found the Madhhij *da'wah* (call) extended to tribes across the erstwhile border: al-Harith, near Bayhan, and Murad, south of Ma'rib, for instance, had always been connected, and now the links were revivified. For the first time in at least twenty years the name Madhhij meant something. More than this, the Madhhij *da'wah* re-emerged in the setting sketched above. First, the belief was widespread that the state was setting tribe against tribe, so this Madhhij identity was invoked in talks with such Bakil tribes as Khawlan al-Tiyal, not simply in continued conflict. Second, the objectification of *al-'adat al-qabaliyyah* (tribal customs) meant that such talks were distinct from the rhetoric of state—a different register, as linguists might say, a language that allows communication despite differences over national politics.

Conferences interweave the two registers, tribe and state. As previously mentioned, such conferences are not wholly new, but formal meetings were a prominent feature of tribal affairs from unity in 1990 to the outbreak of fighting in 1994. They were stimulated in the ways just outlined. At the same time, they appropriated the style of parties and government with a fluency not seen before.

The first major conference was the Solidarity Conference of Yemeni Tribes (*mu'tamar al-tadamun li-l-qaba'il al-yamaniyyah*), convened in early October 1990. A video-tape of the proceedings leaves no doubt as to how big this was. Some thousands of delegates came from all over Yemen, not only from the northern plateau and the Jawf but even from al-Bayda'. The conference expressed particular concern about the expulsion of Yemeni laborers from Saudi Arabia. Its line was broadly sympathetic to the Saudis, most unsympathetic to Iraq.[33] Since the conference apparently received no coverage in the Yemeni press, it is interesting to quote from the resolutions:

3. The meeting condemns Iraqi piracy and aggression against the sister state of Kuwait.

6. Striving for the unity of the Yemeni people, those at the meeting demand that the new united Yemen be placed under the banner of Islam, that Yemen's official position on the Gulf crisis be rectified and that the sons of the Yemeni tribes be allowed to cast themselves into the ranks of the Kuwaiti resistance.

Quite what that might have achieved was not addressed in detail. But any doubt concerning the meeting's position on internal Yemeni affairs was removed by clause 12:

12. Those at the meeting have not ceased to remember with sorrow the slaughter that befell sixty-five shaykhs of Khawlan, including Shaykh Naji bin 'Ali al-Ghadir, Shaykh Salih bin 'Ali al-Hayyal,

Shaykh 'Ali bin Muhammad Hantash and others. And what befell the tribe of 'Abidah. For that we hold responsible partyism [*hizbiyyah*] in general and the YSP in particular.

The shaykhs of Khawlan had been murdered by the Southern government in the early 1970s. Telegrams on the matter were sent to the president: they were never answered.

The conference elected Hamud Abu Ra's as general secretary. Unfortunately, the aims of the conference were less clear than they might have been. Indeed, many tribesmen whose personal liking for Abu Ra's was enormous said this was *siyasah bidun baramij* (politics with no policies). Certain enthusiasts, most notably from Khawlan al-Tiyal, met every question with the slogan, *al-yaman hiya l-qaba'il wa-l-qaba'il hiya l-yaman* (Yemen is the tribes, and the tribes are Yemen). Although there is a grain of truth to the claim, it does not take one far analytically. Nor perhaps should it, for, whatever the inclinations of those involved with the conference, they have not thought it the conference's business to promulgate detailed policy: a position is taken on the great affairs of the day but not on more particular aims, which perhaps would usurp tribal autonomy.

The most important of the documents first issued, in 1990, were therefore probably the (general) Pact of Solidarity (*qa'idat al-tadamun*) and the Summons to Truce (*da'wah li-sulh*). The conference works through what it thinks are cat's-paws.[34] Its membership is dramatically indeterminate. On both counts it is difficult to assess what the conference may or may not have achieved; but the claim that the tribes must solve their own problems, which are caused by hidden hands, is distinctive of the period.

The same concern for truce-making led to the next of the major tribal organizations, the National Cohesion Conference (*mu'tamar al-talahum al-watani*). Its history, briefly, was this. Harashah of al-Mahashimah (part of Dahm) had a long-standing dispute with the *waqf* (Islamic endowment) authorities over land near Sa'dah (note again the theme of dishonest land-deals, supposedly linked to the government apparatus). An attempt at mediation by 'Abdullah Daris failed. A later attempt with a larger delegation, including not only 'Abdullah Daris but 'Abdullah Muhsin Thawabah (also of Dhu Muhammad), made progress. The process snowballed. A much larger delegation was later sent to mediate between Bani Nawf and Al Hamad of Dhu Husayn: this intractable dispute, which over the years had seen almost two hundred people killed, was brought under guaranty by no fewer than eighty Bakil shaykhs with their followers bringing pressure to bear on those at odds for forty-four straight days. A truce was arranged between al-Maranat of Sufyan and al-'Atif of al-Dumaynah (Dhu Muhammad). A long dispute in al-'Amalisah was brought to judgement, another one in Al Salim, another in Al 'Ammar, and so on; a truce was even achieved between Bayt Haydar and Bayt Dhayban in Sufyan (Bakil), although not between Qays and Khiyar of Bani Suraym (Hashid), and never between Bayt Haydar and Bayt al-Ahmar, which might unravel, were it ever solved, disputes the length and breadth of tribal Yemen.[35]

Early in their progress from Barat to San'a', the peace-makers found themselves in broad agreement with other shaykhs from Bakil—with Muhsin Abu Nashtan of Arhab, for instance, who was later thought worth someone shooting at.[36] A meeting of the National Cohesion Conference was convened in December 1991 near Raydah. Regrettably, some effort was made by the president's men to prevent people attending or even finding out what was going on. The conference nevertheless took place and the resolutions were duly published:

1. The resolution of differences in the various parts of the country and clearing up all the tribal and clan law cases, problems and blood-debts. The state is to be the basis for the solution of all such cases . . .

2. Complete equality of rights and duties among all the sons of the people without distinction on the basis of region or tribe . . .

4. The ending of differences and distinctions in benefits and responsibilities within the organizations of our armed forces and internal security forces produced by induction depending on tribal and clan membership and on personal control, which our people utterly reject . . .

The slightly forced term 'clan' here, as opposed to 'tribal', marks *'asha'iriyyah* as opposed to *qabaliyyah*. The use of the term *'asha'iriyyah* was enough to suggest a certain YSP involvement, and any doubt is removed by a reference later in clause 4 to the army and security forces protecting the country's *amn wa istiqrar* (security and stability), which of all YSP catch-phrases was the most persistent and conspicuous. Clause 9 even links this *amn wa istiqrar* with *lijan sha'biyyah* (popular committees) of a type that were standard in the South and unknown in the North.

The connection with the YSP went back to the initial peace-making efforts at Sa'dah, where a Southerner was provincial governor. In so far as that connection developed, however, it was not entirely from choice. Repeated efforts to gain the ear of the president's men were turned down. It was not just the National Cohesion Conference. Several Barat shaykhs (including some who were probably never with this conference)[37] were dismissed by the president's men with the advice to join Shaykh 'Abdullah of Hashid—which at that time failed to address their problems. Messages to the president from the National Cohesion Conference received no more attention than had messages from the very different Solidarity Conference of Yemeni Tribes. San'a' rejected everyone equally, refusing even to talk about the tribes' concerns.

The National Cohesion Conference achieved a great deal. It contained disputes which no one else had been able to manage, some of them dating back for decades, and it began to build a system for tribes to interact with parties without becoming parties themselves. All of this was done by shaykhs who were not closely involved with government. None of these people was a fool. Few were so innocent as to forget the record of the YSP before unity (which Western diplomats and journalists at the time seemed often to forget), and probably fewer still thought of themselves as in any way socialists, any more than did Hizb al-Haqq, the traditionalist Zaydi party which was closely concerned with some of these events.

The Solidarity Conference of Yemeni Tribes had been fiercely anti-socialist. Its sympathy for Saudi Arabia was loudly proclaimed, and its leader met King Fahd and Prince Sultan more than once thereafter. The National Cohesion Conference, by contrast, worked with the socialists easily and many of its members distrusted the Saudis. (That certain of the Saudi leadership preferred 'Ali Salim al-Bid to 'Ali 'Abdullah Salih, regardless of ideology, had not yet sunk in with either group.) The membership overlapped, of course. The leaderships of the two groupings, however, got on less well than some in the National Cohesion Conference might have wished. Almost all they had in common was a distrust of the president's men and of the great shaykhs who dominated the headlines. That distrust seems to have been reciprocated. Both initiatives were conducted by groups of quite ordinary shaykhs, who between them had greater practical influence over tribal affairs throughout the period than did most of the famous names.

The paramount shaykh of Bakil, according to the press, is Naji bin 'Abd al-'Aziz al-Shayif. It is unlikely that he played a part in any of this. In fact, his influence in Bakil at this period was, as it has usually been, minimal. The money that has come his way through the years from north of the border amounts to a tidy sum. Yet in playing these games of patronage, there were surely half a dozen people in Bakil who might have been seen as at least as promising allies. Although one cannot grudge the shaykh his prosperity (*al-rizq min Allah*), one sometimes wonders whether those charged with managing Yemeni affairs understand what they are doing.[38] While the famous names doubtless present themselves to outsiders as commanding tribes, ordinary people in tribal territory invoke tribal values precisely to complain of and avoid their influence. The game of nations is played by rules which are not always those of tribesmen.

On occasion, the responses to state and party actions were self-consciously 'traditional' as well as strongly felt. Naji Bajjash al-Shayif of Dhu Husayn, for instance, was involved with the National Cohesion Conference in its early days and was killed in his house at Barat by Muhammad 'A'id of Dhu Muhammad, who had accompanied him there from San'a'. Muhammad 'A'id was a close confidant of one of the president's brothers. The political implications were felt to be all too clear. People unfamiliar with tribes suggested that Dhu Muhammad and Dhu Husayn would be set at odds. But in fact Dhu Muhammad responded by destroying 'A'id's house and promising to kill him themselves to wipe out the disgrace he had brought on all of them: even now, whatever parties may do, there are things that are simply 'not done' in tribal terms.

The National Cohesion Conference was the major contributor to forming the next large meeting of tribes, the Saba' Conference, which met at Wadi Dhannah—and met deliberately on the anniversary of the North's revolution, thus delivering something of a snub to San'a'. Wadi Dhannah is just within Khawlan's territory. Invitations and statements of safe-conduct were sent specifically by shaykhs of Khawlan, an astute move not only to disarm allegations of party difference but to sidestep accusations of tribal bias.[39] A certain sympathy for the YSP and distrust of the GPC was undoubtedly felt by some of the organizers of the conference, but those who attended entertained a far wider set of views. As had happened with the National Cohesion Conference at Raydah, efforts were made by the president's men to prevent the meeting taking place.[40]

Two *zawamil* (minor poems) give an idea of the meeting's position towards the government:

> Murad said, Shame! Who puts up with a liar's an ass.
> Sanhan's rule's despotic, and all Yemen's produce is theirs.
> They visited the regions, where work in factory or household was made disappointing.
> And we're stuck at home. Disgraceful, they said, if we do what they did.

> All Yemen's income is Sanhan's or else Bin Ahmar's
> The rest of us have gone to ruin.
> The unshaven lad is head of a camp now,
> And hangers-on are the heads of regions.

In the course of the meeting there occurred a significant shift in the leadership. Those who had promoted the meeting most vigorously gave place to a broader coalition and the meeting elected as chairman Muhammad Naji al-Ghadir, who was perhaps more sympathetic to the Saudis than were some of his colleagues.[41] The resolutions passed by the conference, however, were of the same kind as the National Cohesion Conference had published a year earlier:

1. The meeting strongly affirms the profound importance of preserving Yemeni unity and not encroaching upon it . . .

3. The meeting holds the state responsible for all the wars, fighting, bloodshed and political assassinations that have befallen the tribes and the sons of Yemen more generally, considering these to be produced by the state . . .

5. The meeting affirms the state's ultimate responsibility for equality of rights and duties among the different groups of the sons of the people . . .

11. The conferees confirm their rejection of distinctions regarding responsibilities and ranks among the sons of the people in the ranks of the armed forces and security on the basis of family or tribal connections or personal control or party allegiance.

The General Secretariat, whose names appeared at the end of the document, comprised eleven tribal notables.[42] Under the joint leadership of Muhammad al-Ghadir and 'Ali al-Qibli Nimran, the Saba' Conference continued to meet periodically afterwards and to publish statements. Anyone who knows the tribes will agree that this committee cannot be reduced to terms of party allegiance. The spread of tribes involved is impressive. Let me only add that, although many people at the meeting were discontented with Sanhan, none of the principals has ever, in my hearing, so much as mentioned Hashid as a bloc. The newspaper treatment of Hashid and Bakil as homogeneous groupings did not reflect actual practice.[43]

The latest of the major conferences, the United Bakil Conference which met in January 1994, seems at first glance to be a more 'factional' undertaking, insisting on Bakil's taking part in all national organizations by way of the conference (resolution 1/1). Yet even here the stress is on 'preserving the historic, national relation which ties Bakil to all the other Yemeni tribes' (resolution 5), and the form of the resolutions is the same as at the more general conferences. The complaints lodged had simply become a little sharper:

> The Bakil Conference enjoins the authorities to preserve public wealth, not to fritter it away . . .; not to leave public wealth in the hands of an individual or party to use for buying protection or influence; . . . to prevent public funds being spent other than in accordance with the system and laws, as laid down in the state's public budget . . . (resolution 3/1).

The everyday forms of this problem are clear in the following resolution, where the conference demands that the state:

> put an end to extravagant government expenditure on partying [*ihtifalat*], cars, furniture and the travel expenses of individuals; prevent [simply] issuing currency . . .; and ban what are known as 'hidden clauses' . . .

In other words, this is a reference to corruption in business deals. Finance should be administered, according to the resolutions, on the principle of 'Where did you get that from?' (*min ayn laka hadha?*).

Statements from the National Cohesion Conference, the Saba' Conference (latterly, the Conference of Yemeni Tribes) and the Bakil Conference are wide-ranging. There are also resolutions on the budget and economic policy, on education and on the need to support the agricultural sector, as well as on army recruitment and on politics in its simplest forms. (The statements issued by many of these conferences are sophisticated and well thought out.) Although the more interesting resolutions are in abeyance, certain points are worth stressing as common to them all.

First, none makes a claim to tribal precedence. Indeed all of them insist that tribalism is a matter of equality and that promoting people on the grounds of shared tribal membership is wrong. (Obviously, they assume someone else is doing this, otherwise they would not complain; but, quite unlike the resolutions of ten years ago, they do not do it themselves.)

Second, all of them insist on administrative reform. Their complaints, indeed, are similar to those heard from business people. (It is important to remember that everyone is involved in business, from the great with their foreign bank accounts to the small with their shops or their few trucks.)

Third, the disputes and bloodshed that others often blame on the tribes are blamed by all the tribal meetings on the state. (There is reason to agree with them; but the reversal of accusations meant that the tribes were standing together in ways they had not often done before.)

Fourth, reform of the state apparatus is a constant demand, as it has been in many quarters. (Far from rejecting the state, let alone a particular government, the tribes have been demanding that they be treated decently as citizens; there is no doubt whatsoever of their national loyalty.)

Finally, although the party preferences of those involved differ hugely, all the meetings insist upon strict neutrality with regard to party claims. (Tribalism appears as a means of constraining the excesses of factionalism, yet still allows tribespeople to take part freely in the wider forms of national politics.)

In practice, the concern has been to insulate tribesfolk from the consequences of state malfeasance. A conference in al-Bayda' governorate in January 1994 pursued the same line. The tribal component was represented not by some declaration of party allegiance, far less by a tribal claim to precedence, but by a pledge of general truce among all the region's tribes: self-preservation was the pressing need. From that basis it was hoped ultimately to build a more tolerant and fairer state.[44]

Although tribal meetings were the first and the largest, they were followed by regional meetings of broadly the same kind—the Ta'izz Conference and the Hajjah Conference, for instance. None was under party control and certainly none was under the control of the state. If political scientists are still looking for expressions of civil society (the equivalent of Junior Chambers of Commerce, the League of Women Voters and the lost mystique of New England town meetings in the United States), here was part of it for them to study. If the present Yemeni government rhetoric of pluralism, democracy and freedom of speech is meant sincerely, it will be evident from the presence of regional and tribal meetings which act independently. If such meetings disappear, we shall suspect that the rhetoric is only flatulence.[45]

When fighting between the two regionally based parties broke out in May 1994, the assumption in some quarters seemed to be that Bakil, among others, would act as a bloc against the Northern government: reportedly, quantities of guns and money were sent them by people in the South. But Bakil had more sense. So did the Madhhij tribes. So, as we have seen, did areas of the Southern governorates that are spoken of as tribal. Whatever the fantasies of journalists,[46] this unwillingness of the tribes as such to be counters in the game of nations was to be expected. The message of tribal meetings had intensified perhaps, but its tenor was consistent from start to finish, from May 1990 to May 1994.

What is Tribalism?

The Solidarity Conference of Yemeni Tribes (the meeting first convened in 1990) have on their stationery the Quranic line, *ja'alna-kum shu'uban wa-qaba'ila* (We have made you as peoples and as tribes). The division of the world into tribes is the work of God, not man, and is taken as simply being there. Although the identity and composition of particular tribes may change, the fact of tribes is given—which distinguishes this way of looking at the world from the salient Western myth (Hobbes or

The Tribal Factor in the Yemeni Crisis

Rousseau) of starting with pre-social individuals and assuming that society has to be constructed. The 'state of nature' in the tribal view is social from the very outset.

This has practical implications. While parties and state apparatus are seen as creations of particular people, and often as expressions of personal ambition, tribal membership is something everyone has, be they great or small. There is no reason that one tribe should not meet another. Indeed, there is every reason why they should. They have concerns in common and a common language in which to talk. So long as their discussions are in this self-consciously tribal register, political differences within or between tribes are momentarily set aside. The first of the major conferences that we discussed rejected party politics entirely. The later ones took the more productive view that party allegiance was unexceptionable but was simply not the business of the conferences as such to intervene in. For all of them, however, the issue would seem to be less this tribe or that but tribalism as understood by ordinary people, threatened by the recent conduct of state politics.

The question now is whether the country's leaders can respond to such demands for civility. The president is constrained by a system of patronage that has grown steadily for a decade and has distanced him from his natural constituency of support—the tribes not least. To change that will not be easy: it requires statesmanship of a high order. Shaykh 'Abdullah al-Ahmar, for his part, invokes tribal values[47] and decorates his refurbished house with the genealogy of all Qahtan. Unless those older values are taken seriously, however, the names mean little. At the end of the fighting, the government seems more distant from the people than the Presidential Council might wish and there remains a great deal of work to do if Yemen is to be more than just an army and a mass of confused, disaffected citizens. Tribal claims ring hollow.

The mood of tribespeople is caught most exactly by *zawamil* such as those quoted above. Suffice it to say, these circulate everywhere. Their point is taken by people from all the tribes, regardless of where the listeners come from: Hashid, Bakil, Madhhij or any other tribe. But not everyone has been producing these *zawamil* on political subjects. The supposed tribal 'key' to events, Hashid, has been conspicuous for its silence. It is as if Hashidis—caught between the dominance of a very few of their number and the problems most of them share with their tribal neighbors—find their own position unintelligible in tribal terms.

CHAPTER THREE

Internal Politics in Yemen: Recovery or Regression?

Charles F. Dunbar

The victory of San'a' in Yemen's 1994 civil war can be seen either as a brilliant achievement or as a catastrophic failure of national policy. Viewed in one way, the war was the final triumph of Yemeni nationalism over a selfish few within the country bent on personal gain, and over outside forces seeking to avenge themselves for Yemen's refusal to join the coalition against Saddam Hussein and above all to keep Yemen weak. From this perspective, the defeat of former Vice-President 'Ali Salim al-Bid and his Yemeni Socialist Party (YSP) cohorts is the last stage of a process begun in 1962 with the establishment of the Yemen Arab Republic (YAR) and leading, after much adversity and many setbacks, to the emergence once and for all of a united and republican Yemen.

This version of events is open to challenge. The case can be made that the war, with its exchanges of Scud missiles, destruction of property and loss of civilian life, was a disastrous setback for a country whose political fortunes had been on the rise. In the spring of 1990, enthusiasm for unity under what was then seen as an increasingly democratic regime was high, particularly in the South, and President 'Ali 'Abdullah Salih's headlong drive towards unity was praised as a brilliant act of political vision. Even after the Gulf war and the economic setback represented by the return of some 800,000 Yemeni workers from Saudi Arabia, Yemen's parliamentary elections in the spring of 1993 were hailed in the West as a triumph for democracy.

Instead of consolidating its gains, however, San'a' left the South to its own limited devices, did little to remove or reform the old socialist bureaucracy, and appeared to spend outside the South its modest income from the growing oil production, including that generated in the Southern province of Hadramawt. Thus, when the Southern leaders decided to go it alone, they were able to command the loyalty of the former South Yemeni military establishment and at least the tacit acceptance of a Southern populace which two years earlier had appeared glad to be seeing the last of Yemeni socialism. In the North, many major political leaders, particularly of the tribes, quickly distanced themselves from President Salih and, according to San'a', made common cause with his enemies, both domestic and foreign.

The civil war of 1994, the argument concludes, was the inevitable result of San'a''s inaction and incompetence. It erased any vestiges of Southern goodwill towards San'a', left the country bitterly divided, and reduced to vanishing point the chance of President Salih's being either able or willing to lead the country towards political pluralism and economic well-being.

The Yemeni reality appears to be a blend of the positive and negative arguments outlined above. Whatever his popularity, 'Ali 'Abdullah Salih is once more the undisputed leader of his country, in all likelihood popular within his victorious army and in full control of the South's valuable natural resources. San'a''s victory has also consolidated Yemeni unity and bought the government time to make the union beneficial to all Yemenis. At the same time, President Salih's enemies, while likely to lie low in the short term, are still on or near the scene, and other political figures, like the Northern tribal leaders who left him to his own devices when his political fortunes were at a low ebb, may well turn on him if they perceive his grip on power to be weakening. Inaction, or the perception of inaction, on San'a''s part in dealing with the country's economic ills could lead to one of the abrupt changes in regime for which Yemen, both North and South, has been noted.

In the following pages, the writer hazards some guesses about the likely course of Yemeni domestic politics for the remainder of the twentieth century. The likelihood that the present alignment of political forces will be preserved is first assessed. Next, the prospects for any of four forces for political change gaining ascendancy over the others and altering the status quo are considered. The chapter concludes with a few thoughts about policies which could prolong the life of the present

Internal Politics in Yemen: Recovery or Regression?

government and about the chances for such policies being pursued.

Five Scenarios

In looking at Yemen's political prospects over the course of the next few years, it is possible to identify five directions in which the country could move. The first, and in the writer's view most likely, course is the maintenance of what in a less than stable situation may be termed the status quo. Four other, much less probable lines of political development are: a resurgence of tribalism and the consequent weakening of central government authority; the emergence of a radical Islamist state; a revival of the North–South division; and a genuine liberalization of the country's political system. Elements of two or more of these scenarios could, of course, be present at the same time; resurgent tribalism and a revived North–South conflict, for example, could very likely go hand in hand. There could also be a mix between authoritarianism and political liberalization; the nature of the mix would depend on the self-confidence of the government in San'a'. Nevertheless, for the purposes of analysis, it is useful to consider each political force or tendency separately.

The Status Quo

In the near and middle term, there are compelling reasons to believe that Yemen's political physiognomy will remain essentially as it is now. As at present, the regime is likely to be authoritarian, with President Salih, aided by a few trusted advisers and with the army and security services standing behind him, calling all the major political shots. Military spending may be expected to remain high, both to deter tribal opposition and as a means of retaining the loyalty of the armed forces.

The trappings of democracy which existed before the civil war are likely to reappear, but with significant limitations. As before, the parliament and other elected bodies may be expected to have a major say on matters such as the budget. However, the important freedoms of speech and the press that Yemenis gained before the war will very likely be restricted at least in the short run. President Salih is also unlikely to change his preference for negotiation and reconciliation, rather than confrontation, in dealing with actual or potential political opponents. So far, he has given every indication that he will let bygones be bygones with the Northern tribal leaders who failed to stand by him during the confrontation with the Southern leadership. He is also engaged in a bargaining process with the Islamists, who supported him during the war and who now want more concessions and influence than he is prepared to give them. Finally, with the exception of the principal leaders of the South, 'Ali Salih has offered an amnesty which may eventually be accepted by Southerners who are still suspicious of his willingness and ability to let them re-enter the country and, perhaps eventually, public life.

Among the reasons for believing that the status quo will be preserved, President Salih's personality and political position are perhaps the most obvious. First and foremost, he has just won a war in which the popular cause of Yemeni unity had been called into question. His Southern foes are in some cases dead and in most others abroad. The Bakil confederation tribal leaders—who, according to one of his closest advisers, plotted against him—and even his fellow Hashid tribal confederation shaykh, Mujahid Abu Shawarib, stayed on the sidelines during the war. They bear the political liability of failing to back the unionist cause. In 1990 'Ali Salih gambled on unity and won. In 1991 he played the weak hand he dealt himself in the Gulf war and survived. In 1994 he defied the conventional wisdom that neither the North nor the South could defeat the other and emerged victorious in a high-stakes fight which few believed he could win and in which outside powers were urging him to cut his losses and accept the *fait accompli* of Southern secession.

In this situation, it is unlikely that President Salih will change his basic style of governing. On the one hand, he has been an authoritarian leader for sixteen years and has survived, and at times even prospered, when others before him have lost at least their jobs and sometimes their lives. His experience in the past year would seem unlikely to have changed his view that his political and physical survival depends on his ability to rule with a strong hand.

At the same time, the run-up to the civil war showed President Salih once more that he has many powerful enemies whom it is better to placate, and if possible co-opt, rather than confront. Particularly in the present unsettled political times, it is unlikely that he will choose to try to settle scores with those who opposed him. Indeed, a close adviser to 'Ali Salih has indicated that the government intends to resume business as usual with almost all the tribal leaders who either opposed the

Internal Politics in Yemen: Recovery or Regression?

president or remained neutral during the war.[1]

Another element helping to preserve the status quo is the high propensity of Yemenis to bow to the will of a strong leader like 'Ali Salih on major questions of national policy. Despite the misgivings of conservatives in the North about unification with the 'godless' South and the hardship caused by President Salih's tilt towards Iraq in the Gulf war, there was virtually no criticism of either policy in public, and few Yemenis were prepared to be critical even in private conversation. While this reticence stemmed in considerable measure from fear of security service reprisals, it also reflected a strong tendency on the part of Yemenis to leave high politics to their leaders, particularly to one who had succeeded as well as the president. This attitude may be expected to strengthen his hand as he sets his post-war political course.

There are two areas in which the government's authoritarian tendencies may be expected to grow. First, it is likely that the intelligence services will be given a freer hand to seek out and neutralize perceived threats to state security. The president's close adviser has made clear the belief that plotting against the government was widespread. Particularly as scores are settled in the immediate aftermath of the war, individual liberties may be expected to take a back seat to security concerns. A case in point is the reported jailing of journalists and intellectuals in mid-July 1994 following a public meeting to discuss the country's future.[2]

Second, the government is almost certain to make major changes in the administrative structure in the South. In the four years between unification and the civil war, the YSP was left largely in control of the Southern bureaucracy. This, according to the president's adviser cited above, not only impeded efforts at economic liberalization but assured a large measure of support both for the YSP in the 1993 elections and for the Southern leaders in the run-up to the civil war. A priority for the government in San'a', according to the adviser, will be to install administrators loyal to it in all areas of the Southern bureaucracy.

Before analyzing the political forces which could challenge a continuation of President Salih's authoritarian rule, it is worth asking whether that system could survive if he were removed from the scene, most probably by assassination. The sudden disappearance of the head of state would, of course, produce political turbulence, and it is questionable whether the constitutional procedure for presidential succession would be followed beyond the very short term. At the same time, it is likely that the armed forces would involve themselves in the succession and that they would try to establish an authoritarian regime similar to that of the president. While it is not clear that they would prevail in a post-Salih power struggle, the armed forces appear to be at least as well placed as other elements in the society, such as the tribes or the Islamists, to influence the outcome.

In sum, President Salih has emerged from the war with a substantial short-term ability to continue his authoritarian rule, and the regime he has created could conceivably survive his sudden departure from the scene. How short that term turns out to be will depend both on his ability to deal with Yemen's various woes and on the degree to which politics and society in Yemen could be organized along other lines. Four such ways are considered below, and the likelihood of their gaining currency assessed.

Tribal Resurgence

The tribes of Yemen have played a major role in shaping the country's destiny, but their political power *vis-à-vis* that of the government in San'a' has been in decline over the past fifteen years. Prior to the establishment of the YAR in 1962, the tribes managed most aspects of everyday life throughout the country with the imamate playing a limited role. In the Republic's first two decades, the tribal leaders like 'Abdullah bin Husayn al-Ahmar, paramount shaykh of the Hashid confederation, shaped the country's political destiny. During much of this period, the government's writ in the tribal areas in the north and east of the YAR did not extend much beyond the limits of its few large towns.

Throughout most of the 1980s, the major political dynamic in the YAR was the gradual expansion of government authority into the tribal areas and the consequent decline in the political power of the tribal leaders. By delivering social services such as schools, clinics and roads to the tribal areas, the government became a rival to the shaykhs and at the same time began co-opting them by giving them lucrative business opportunities. In this way, men such as Sinan Abu Lahum, paramount shaykh of the Nihm tribe in the Bakil confederation, became more devoted to their business interests and less to maintaining their positions within their tribes. Some formally abandoned their leadership positions in the tribe to devote themselves full time to the making of money.

This is not to say that conflict between government and tribes disappeared in the 1980s or that President Salih no longer needed to take such disputes seriously. In the late 1980s the president cut short a state visit to China and returned home when his Sanhan tribe of the Hashid confederation fell to fighting with the neighboring Khawlan group of the Bakil. Also, in 1989, he worked assiduously to resolve a stand-off between government forces and tribes in the eastern province of Ma'rib. Hijackings of oil company vehicles and kidnapping of tourists and oil company workers in Ma'rib and, to a lesser extent, in Sa'dah in the north periodically get out of hand and, when they do, the government in San'a' quickly becomes involved.

In none of these conflicts, however, has the growing ability of the government to operate in most of the country's tribal areas been seriously called into question. This is true in part because President Salih has not allowed them to fester but rather has moved quickly to contain them with temporary truces. These improvised solutions have tended to become permanent with the passage of time. The failure of such disputes to develop into serious problems for the government is a reflection of the growing power and influence of the state *vis-à-vis* that of the tribal leaders.

If ever there was a golden opportunity for tribal leaders disgruntled with President Salih to regain their former political prominence, it was represented by the 1994 civil war. The threat to the government in San'a' posed by an apparently well-supplied and well-financed Southern army was the most dangerous it had faced since coming into existence in 1962. Further, it was widely reported and believed that the government of Saudi Arabia was ready to cooperate with disgruntled tribal leaders in order to weaken President Salih's government. The president's adviser cited above asserted that many prominent shaykhs had been in contact both with the Saudis and with the Southern leaders to plan antigovernment strategy. Finally, it was widely reported in the media that the Bakil confederation was prepared to follow the time-honored tribal practice of laying siege to San'a', as was done during the civil war in the 1960s, in support of the Southern effort.

For at least three reasons, the tribal threat to the government in San'a' did not materialize. First, the Bakil leaders appeared unable or unwilling to work together against President Salih's government. Links among Bakil confederation tribes are looser than they are in Hashid, and the nominal paramount shaykh of Bakil, Naji al-Shayif of Dhu Muhammad, does not play the same prominent role in tribal and national politics as his Hashid opposite number, Shaykh 'Abdullah bin Husayn al-Ahmar. Shaykh Naji was also in difficulties because of his alleged involvement in an attempt to assassinate a prominent Northern politician. Second, Shaykh 'Abdullah, whose Hashid fighters had been active in fighting against the South in the 1979 border war, remained loyal to San'a' and his conservative political party, the Yemeni Reform Grouping (YRG or Islah), actively supported the government against the South. Lastly, Mujahid Abu Shawarib, the prominent Hashidi shaykh mentioned above, while apparently disenchanted with the government, chose simply to leave the country during the war. Had he given more support to the rebellion, Hashidi solidarity with the government might have been broken.

Thus, the 1994 civil war seems to have reaffirmed the view that the ability of Yemen's tribal leaders to play a determining role in national politics continues to decline as the military and economic power of the government has grown. Had San'a' been forced to sue for peace in the war, the tribal leaders might have tried to mount a serious challenge to President Salih. With the outcome of the fighting in doubt, however, they were apparently not prepared to take him on and San'a''s victory has, if anything, strengthened the government's hand for future dealings with the tribes.

Islamic Radicalism
A second force which is theoretically capable of challenging the government is the country's Islamist movement, at whose center is the YRG. Having won nearly 25% of the vote in the 1993 elections, and with one of its most prominent leaders, Shaykh 'Abd al-Majid al-Zindani, installed as a member of the five-man Presidential Council, the YRG was a natural ally of the government in its war against the former communist leaders of the South. The international media, ever alert for signs of the rise of 'Islamic fundamentalism' in another Muslim country, focused on the alleged presence in the ranks of the Northern army of Islamist irregular troops and on the reported destruction of the beer factory following Aden's fall. Irregular troops loyal to the YRG, with returners from the war in Afghanistan among them, are said to have fought bravely during the civil war.

On the face of it, the YRG is indeed a force to be reckoned with. Its radical Islamist wing, represented by men such as al-Zindani, has for a number of years preached a militant Islamist message in the country's mosques and in the 'scientific institutes' which offer a heavily religious curriculum as an alternative to the government-run secondary schools. With Shaykh 'Abdullah bin Husayn al-Ahmar at its head, the YRG is also a natural political home for the Northern tribes who find its resolutely anti-communist and ultra-conservative position appealing. The YRG's third dimension is the support it receives from many of the country's wealthy businessmen, whose financial backing is as important to the grouping as it is to political movements elsewhere.

In the weeks following the end of the civil war, the YRG began to flex its political muscles. It was widely reported to be demanding a second seat on the five-man Presidential Council, filling one of the two held previously by the YSP. The YRG also walked out of the post-war cabinet meeting held in Aden as a gesture of reconciliation on July 14, because a Southern minister who had rallied to San'a"s cause during the fighting had been reinstated and allowed to attend. The YRG's position is said to be that, while ex-communists could be forgiven the error of their previous ways at the time of unification, their decision either to join al-Bid's efforts openly or to sit on the sidelines should exclude them from a future political role in Yemen. Finally, it was reported that a YRG member appointed to a provincial post in the South during or immediately after the war immediately dismissed two of his subordinates who were members of the YSP.[3]

For three sets of reasons, the YRG does not appear capable at present of imposing a radical Islamist agenda on Yemen. First, more than Islamist parties in other parts of the Muslim world, the YRG is a broad coalition of people with differing views and interests, not a disciplined party with a well-defined political doctrine. The party's tribal and business elements are basically conservative with a considerable stake in preserving a status quo which brings them great economic and political benefit.

Second, the government and its ruling party, the General People's Congress (GPC), have had some success at stealing the YRG's political thunder. The GPC has taken a conservative position on social issues such as polygamy and the sale of alcohol. Despite its unwillingness until recently to accept the demand that Islam be the 'sole' rather than the 'principal' basis of Yemen's law, the conservative religious credentials of the GPC and the government have been hard for the YRG to challenge.[4]

Finally, the elements needed to bring about an Islamist revolution do not appear to be present in Yemen as yet. Unlike many states with strong Islamist movements, Yemen is still a largely rural country, and the large groups of disaffected young men from the countryside who have been the shock troops of radical Islamist activity in Tehran, Cairo and Algiers are not yet present in its cities. Further, Yemen does not have a large body of unemployed, poorly educated 'intellectuals' from whom Islamist movements elsewhere have drawn support.

The underlying theme in the preceding paragraph stresses that Islamic radicalism could become a major force in Yemen in the mid-term and beyond. In San'a', the YRG appears to be gaining ground, notably at San'a' University where its threats to secular professors have prompted some to seek employment outside the country.[5] At the same time, the safety valve for Yemeni manpower was closed when the Yemeni workers returned from Saudi Arabia during the Gulf crisis, and the country's universities are producing a growing crop of ersatz intellectuals. Both groups will be drawn to the cities and, in the absence of significant economic development, are as likely as their brethren elsewhere to embrace radical Islam. As the size of these disaffected groups increases, a truly radical Islamist grouping may be expected to emerge.

Southern Separatism

Despite its military defeat, there are some reasons for believing that Southern separatism will continue. In general, the South has benefited little from unity and, barring a major, government-led economic development effort, disaffection with San'a' is likely to increase. Hadramawt province, with its oilfield and substantial ties to Saudi Arabia, could be the focus of a separatist movement which the Hadrami leaders of the failed movement could be expected to support. While the future policies of regional states like Saudi Arabia are neither clear nor within the purview of this chapter, recent history suggests that a robust separatist movement would receive outside help.

Under present circumstances, however, the re-emergence of a separatist movement in the near term seems unlikely. Exiled Yemeni leaders, whether Southern or Northern, have been notably unsuccessful in re-establishing their popular support within the country. The former Southern leader, 'Ali Nasir Muhammad, is only one example. Further, if San'a' pursues reconciliation as vigorously as a close presidential adviser says is intended, potential separatist leaders may opt for co-optation.

Most important, the strength of popular support for unity would make the revival of a separatist movement a daunting task. It is widely believed that the key error of the South was to declare the establishment of the 'Democratic Republic of Yemen'. Even though the declaration claimed that the new entity represented the whole country and that its leaders would work for Yemeni unity, the Southern leaders were seen to be backing a two-state solution to the civil war and the popularity of their cause suffered accordingly. While their extent is unknown, defections by Southern military units to the Northern cause following the announcement of the new state were significant, and support for San'a' and President Salih certainly increased.[6]

If Southern separatism is not an immediate security problem for San'a' and President Salih, it costs him political capital by denying him potentially valuable allies. Were Yemen's drastic economic decline to continue, Southern separatist sentiment would certainly grow, but the Islamists, not the Southerners, would be better placed to challenge Salih's leadership. The problem for the president is that, if he cannot rebuild his relationship with the Southern leaders and deliver the economic goods to the South, separatist sentiment will deny him the ally he used effectively to counter Islamist influence from 1990 to 1993 and perhaps fatally weaken his presidency over the long run.

A Democratic Opening
Finally, the prospects for a real democratic opening may be briefly considered. President Salih received high marks in the West by holding national elections and taking the unusual step of declaring that he would limit his own term in office. Particularly if accompanied by a generous measure of national reconciliation, new parliamentary elections could give him, fresh from a successful effort to 'save the nation', a renewed mandate for governing the country. Properly managed, the transition to a more participatory political system in Yemen could be accelerated.

Although theoretically possible, it seems unlikely that San'a' will embark on a major democratic opening in the near future. As noted above, President Salih's adviser was obviously preoccupied with the extent of the 'plotting' against the government prior to the civil war. 'Ali Salih may make a genuine effort to bring back into the fold as many of the Southern leaders as possible and re-establish good or at least correct relations with the tribal shaykhs who opposed (or at least did not support) him in his hour of need. He may also permit a gradual relaunching of Yemen's slow progress towards political pluralism and the respect for individual rights and freedoms. Any more ambitious democratic opening is unlikely for some time. President Salih's experience in a turbulent political career inclines him towards the authoritarian methods which have led him to where he now stands.

Conclusions

Yemen's interests have been well served by San'a''s victory in the 1994 civil war. Any other scenario would have been likely to produce a prolonged period of instability, with President Salih fighting for his political life against the tribal leaders whose influence he had been successful in reducing. In such a situation, the prospects for dealing with the North's economic woes would have been poor, and the ability of the South to prosper with the North in turmoil would have been limited.

Thus, as was the case after unification in 1990, the president and the government in San'a' have gained a new lease of political life. The end of the 1994 war may come to be remembered as a turning-point in the tumultuous history of republican Yemen. It is also possible that San'a''s triumph will in time be seen only as a breather for a country doomed to perpetual political infighting and periodic military outbursts. What San'a' does in the months ahead depends largely on which scenario becomes reality.

In this situation, there are three policy lines which the government could usefully pursue. The first, as indicated above, is to seek as broad a measure of national reconciliation as possible. The Yemenis have excelled in this domain; indeed, one Western observer noted that, precisely because they are so poor at conflict avoidance, Yemenis need to have created good mechanisms for conflict resolution. After the civil war in the 1960s, republicans and royalists were able for the most part to overcome their differences and have coexisted more or less peacefully for years. The present animosities between North and South are no more severe than those of the 1960s, and the adviser to President Salih cited above insists that, while the government will avoid any measure which could be construed as recognition of the continued existence of a Southern state, national reconciliation is an absolute policy priority for San'a'.

Internal Politics in Yemen: Recovery or Regression?

Whatever its intentions, San'a' has so far made little progress in its effort to bring Southern leaders back into the united fold. The meeting of the YSP leadership held in Damascus was reportedly disappointed to learn from an emissary sent by President Salih that he could make no promises about the political future of Southern leaders who might respond to his call to return to Yemen. One of those present at the meeting asserted that President Salih was unable to make the gestures needed to achieve national reconciliation because of the power both of the YRG and of conservative Northern figures, including members of his own family.[7]

A second policy imperative—that of economic development—will be harder for the government to pursue. San'a' badly needs to reduce the level of its military expenditure, reportedly one of the highest in the world in per capita terms,[8] to focus on maximizing its income from oil and hopefully from natural gas, and to put these revenues to work in improving the standard of living throughout the country, and particularly in the South. With 350,000 barrels per day of oil production, and a population of only 12-14 million, and with excellent fisheries and moderately good agriculture, Yemen has a potential far greater than that of many other countries. San'a' should be able finally to translate that potential into the reality of a better life for most Yemenis.

For several reasons, President Salih will find this hard to do. First, he is deeply beholden to his armed forces (key elements of which are commanded by his closest relatives) for winning the civil war and is likely to feel a strong compulsion to reward those who stood by him by maintaining a high level of military spending. Keeping the security forces strong will, in any case, suit his authoritarian proclivities and his understandable fear of troublemakers inside the country and out. Furthermore, the problem of how to employ the 800,000 returned workers from Saudi Arabia, most of whom have few prospects of finding jobs outside the country, is one that will defy solution in the short run. Even with the best of will, it will take years before the country's economy can absorb these workers and give them the standard of living they were able to provide for their families before 1990. Despite these difficulties, 'Ali 'Abdullah Salih must address the task of putting Yemen's economic house in order. Failure to do so is likely to be more costly in political terms than trying seriously to break out of economic stagnation.

Finally, while he is unlikely to abandon his authoritarian approach to government, President Salih should return as quickly as possible to the policy of maximizing political pluralism through such measures as allowing a free press, the functioning of political parties and the holding of elections at the national and local levels. Such steps, of course, will burnish Yemen's image with the international financial institutions capable of helping San'a' deal with the country's economic ills. They should also help President Salih consolidate the measure of popularity his victory in the civil war has won him.

The near-term political prospect is for more of the same authoritarian rule which has been Yemen's lot since the establishment of the Republic. To the extent that President Salih can temper his focus on security issues and the strengthening of his armed forces with a concern for economic development and greater political participation, the likelihood of avoiding further crises like the 1994 civil war will increase. The government now has some room for maneuver. Failure to act will narrow its options in the future.

CHAPTER FOUR

The Yemeni Civil War of 1994: Impact on the Arab Gulf States

Robert D. Burrowes

The Yemeni civil war of 1994 ended in early July with the victory of the Northern forces led by President 'Ali 'Abdullah Salih, thereby reaffirming the Republic of Yemen as territorially defined at the time of unification in 1990.[1] The former South Yemen suffered a political-military defeat, probably a definitive one, and those Gulf Cooperation Council (GCC) states that to varying degrees and for varied motives supported the South and its cause were dealt a diplomatic-political defeat.[2]

The Yemeni civil war has consequences for the politics of the Arabian peninsula and for the security of the UAE and the other Arab Gulf states, and these consequences are for the most part negative. The effects of the civil war on these states need not be either great or irreversible. They can be undone, if these states and Yemen want to undo them and are prepared to do quickly what their undoing requires.

Effects of the Civil War

What are these likely effects or consequences? What impact might we expect? My guess is that the politics of the peninsula and the security of the Arab Gulf states could be affected by at least three changes:

(i) There will be a stronger, more united, less dependent Yemen, one more able than before to be unfriendly to neighbors that are unfriendly to it.

(ii) The relationship between Saudi Arabia and Yemen, a complex, ambiguous, half-hidden mix of conflict and cooperation during the 1970s and 1980s, has already become more openly and intensely conflictual and could settle into a cold war pattern with a potential for open warfare, conditions that would surely impact negatively upon the other states on the peninsula.

(iii) The informal, largely inchoate balance-of-power system that emerged on the Arabian peninsula in the 1960s and functioned through the 1980s, one that afforded the Arab Gulf states some relief from pressure from an expansive, often overbearing Saudi Arabia, could become less operable due to new rigidities in relations between Yemen and both Saudi Arabia and these other Gulf states.

Post-War Yemen
Regarding the first change, the Yemen of the second half of the 1990s will closely resemble neither the old image of North Yemen nor the image of Yemen fabricated by the Southerners and their friends abroad. North Yemen—i.e. the Yemen Arab Republic (YAR)—was long perceived as a weak and disorganized country, backward and conservative as well as dependent and desperately poor; it was contrasted with the also very poor, but more progressive, much better organized and disciplined Marxist South Yemen—the People's Democratic Republic of Yemen (PDRY). During the political-military crisis of 1994, the Southern leadership and their friends reworked these images and conjured up the picture of a modern, vibrant, forward-looking, non-socialist South Yemen set against a parochial, backward North Yemen in which progress and development were stifled by the grip of the tribes and Islamic fundamentalism.[3]

The reality of the situation is quite different. The outcome of the civil war should allow finally for the long-delayed merger of the two Yemeni states and their armies. It should also allow for the reorganization of Yemen's political life—hopefully based on the freedoms and multi-party pluralism that flourished during the transition period after unification in 1990. Even in the unlikely event of the guerrilla war promised by the South, the regime headed by President

The Yemeni Civil War of 1994: Impact on the Arab Gulf States

Salih should be able to assert considerable control over most of Yemen. If so, the result will be the most populous state on the Arabian peninsula, one endowed with modest but adequate oil and gas resources and considerable development potential.[4] The YAR, despite its many problems and shortcomings, made important strides under President Salih towards realizing this potential in the 1980s, and there is no compelling reason to believe that the Republic of Yemen cannot do as well. Whether Yemen be unitary or federal, the full incorporation of the 'Southern provinces', especially modern Aden and Hadramawt, will make even less likely the vastly exaggerated threat of a conservative, tribal, Islamist turning away from efforts at modern nation-state building and socio-economic development.

The likelihood that Yemen will soon be a more formidable force in the politics of the Arabian peninsula should pose no direct threat to the UAE and the other Arab Gulf states. Yemen shares a common border with none of the other Arab Gulf states (except Oman) and, even if it wanted to, lacks the ability to project what power it has as far as the Gulf. Its relations with neighboring Oman before the civil war, based upon a major border agreement, could well serve as a model of friendly, mutually beneficial ties. Alarmist critics to the contrary, Yemen will probably have no need, and is probably too wise, to allow itself to be drawn into regional schemes by pariahs like Iraq, Iran and Sudan in the second half of the 1990s—especially if it is afforded an alternative to political isolation on the peninsula. These countries have given no indication of an urge to export their democratic republicanism, except by example. What a stronger Yemen will be able to do, however, is to grant or deny diplomatic-political support if and when it is needed by the UAE and the other Arab Gulf states. It will have the power to be unfriendly and not forthcoming to requests for help.

Worsened Yemeni-Saudi Relations
The deterioration of relations between Yemen and Saudi Arabia since the beginning of the Gulf crisis in 1990 has been dramatic. Moderated somewhat in 1992 and 1993, the exchange of public accusations and criticism rose in 1991 and again in 1994 to levels not heard since the years of the first Yemeni civil war in the 1960s. As a consequence, the simmering undercurrent of conflict between Yemen and Saudi Arabia in the 1970s and 1980s—rooted both in the fears of the Saudi government[5] regarding a strong Yemen and in poor, weak Yemen's resentment

over efforts by Saudi Arabia to use its vast wealth to divide, control and render Yemen dependent—is finally out in the open—and the gloves are off as never before.[6] The Yemenis say that the Saudis opposed unification in 1990, sabotaged it by destroying the economy when they expelled some 800,000 Yemeni workers during the Gulf crisis, and then encouraged and supported the Southern effort in 1994, materially as well as morally. In short, the Yemenis have deeply felt grievances. For their part, the Saudis refuse to forgive the Yemenis for their stand during the Gulf crisis and, more important, regard a unified Yemen possessed of oil resources and bearing a semblance of multi-party pluralist rule as a dangerous, untrustworthy neighbor.

Yemeni-Saudi conflict is made so potentially explosive by virtue of the facts that they are next-door neighbors and share long disputed borders. More than pride of sovereignty, what invests the border disputes with significance is the fact that some of the borderlands may contain oil that the Yemenis sorely need and the Saudis would like to deny them. Since 1990, moreover, the growing hostility between Yemen and Saudi Arabia over other issues has tended increasingly to transfer to and be expressed in terms of the border disputes. Consequently, the stakes have risen and the lines have been drawn more sharply on these disputes. For example, Yemeni claims on 'Asir, Najran and Jizan—claims that had lain dormant for decades—are now being made on the basis of the legal argument that the mass expulsion of Yemenis from Saudi Arabia in 1990 constituted an abrogation of the Ta'if Treaty of 1934, the treaty under which Yemen had suspended its claim to these 'northern provinces'. Having put the issue in play, some Yemeni leaders nonetheless were saying unofficially in the autumn of 1992 that they would be willing to relinquish claims to these areas if the Saudis were forthcoming and generous regarding Yemeni territorial claims in the east and north of Hadramawt. Since then, however, the issue has become so politically charged that it is doubtful whether either side would be able to make such a deal, even if still willing.[7]

Events springing from the border disputes, future Saudi support for a guerrilla war by the South or some other issue could escalate into armed conflict and even war between Saudi Arabia and Yemen. Neither country is prepared for this eventuality. Despite the Gulf war and the 1994 Yemeni civil war, these two states have not had much experience in fighting wars; more important, they have not had much experience in avoiding war and in getting out of wars. Hence, miscalculations and errors are likely. If the hostility between the two largest states on the Arabian peninsula did spin out of control and result in serious armed conflict or war, then it is likely that the neighboring Arab Gulf states would become involved to some degree, through their membership in the GCC or otherwise.[8] For example, conflict between Yemen and Saudi Arabia over Saudi-supported guerrilla activity aimed at Yemen could easily spill over into neighboring Oman.

Rigidified Peninsular Relations
The bloc-like pattern of Saudi Arabia and the other GCC states versus Yemen, a pattern forged in the Gulf crisis in 1990–91 and then reinforced during the political-military crisis in Yemen in 1994, was not the normal political configuration on the Arabian peninsula during the previous quarter century. What distinguished these formative decades of modern Arabia, only to be largely overridden by the politics of the 1990s, was a slowly emergent, somewhat inchoate balance-of-power system. This system had four main features:

(i) modern Saudi Arabia, facing north and east, the hegemonic power reaching out from the center of the peninsula to its periphery, seeking to influence if not control the other Arab Gulf states on matters deemed relevant to the security of the Saudi government;

(ii) Saudi Arabia, again for security reasons, attempting to neutralize Yemen (or the Yemens) to its rear by keeping them weak, divided and (in the case of North Yemen) dependent;

(iii) the neighboring Arab Gulf states trying to lessen Saudi pressure on them by, among other things, strengthening Yemen (or the Yemens) as a check on or a counterweight to the Saudis;[9] and

(iv) Yemen (or the Yemens) seeking aid and support from a variety of sources.

This system operated on a simple logic:

(i) For the Saudis, if Yemen was no longer a worry, they could focus on the challenge of revolutionary Arab nationalism, the excesses of the Kuwaiti legislature, their border disputes with Gulf neighbors, etc.

(ii) For the neighboring Arab Gulf states, if Saudi Arabia were concerned about and preoccupied with Yemen, then the pressure on them eased and they had some breathing space, some room to maneuver.

(iii) For the two Yemens, if they received material and other aid from the Arab Gulf oil states and elsewhere, and if they had good inter-Yemeni relations or even united into one Yemen, then they would be better able to resist Saudi efforts to control or neutralize them.

The logic of balance and countervailing power, when in force as it often was, served to provide the Arab Gulf states with some leverage in their dealings with the much stronger Saudi Arabia. The use of Yemen as a counterweight to Saudi power was most clearly seen in the Saudi-Kuwaiti-Yemeni triangular relationship during the twenty-five years prior to 1990. It helps explain why the newly independent Kuwait gave so much aid to the YAR during the Yemeni civil war in the 1960s, and did so over the objections of the Saudis, who were strongly backing the royalists against the republicans; it also helps explain the continuation of this aid through the 1970s and 1980s, a period in which the Saudis periodically placed considerable pressure on the Kuwaitis to follow their lead and to pursue a more conservative line at home and abroad. Finally, Kuwaiti aid to the Marxist PDRY in the 1970s and 1980s was surely extended in part with an eye towards keeping Saudi Arabia preoccupied with the other side—the Yemeni side—of the Arabian peninsula.

There are many other examples of efforts to befriend and bolster Yemen as a counterbalance to Saudi Arabia. The considerable aid given to the YAR by Abu Dhabi in the 1970s and 1980s probably owes much to this political calculus. Oman's efforts to improve relations with both the YAR and the PDRY in the 1980s can be seen as part of its effort to maintain a measure of autonomy from Saudi Arabia. Finally, the major efforts by the neighboring Arab Gulf states to maintain strong bilateral ties with the YAR in the 1980s were probably intended partly to counter efforts by the Saudis to coordinate if not dominate peninsular affairs through the newly created GCC.

Traces of this system of balance and countervailing power survived the Gulf crisis, down to and even during the Yemeni civil war of 1994. The Saudis were generous in their successful border negotiations with

Oman in the early 1990s, probably in part because they wanted to clear the decks for what promised to be much more important and challenging border talks with Yemen; similarly, the Omanis seemed to play along with subsequent Yemeni attempts to publicize the Yemen–Oman border agreement of 1992 and thereby use it as a way of putting pressure on the Saudis to negotiate in good faith on their border issues. Finally, Qatar's continued good relations with Yemen and its refusal to side with the South during the civil war in 1994 can be traced directly to its border conflict and other problems with Saudi Arabia.

The possibility that the Yemeni civil war will increase both Saudi-Yemeni conflict and the vulnerability of the neighboring Arab Gulf states to Saudi pressure in the second half of the 1990s is made more worrying by Saudi Arabia's new assertiveness in external relations and by the increasing vulnerability of the government of Saudi Arabia to strong and conflicting domestic political forces. In the past, Saudi Arabia's great oil wealth and traditional political infrastructure combined to give the Saudi government the freedom to act externally in a deliberate, moderate way and with a long-term perspective—and it often did so. In contrast to this, the Saudi rulers in the Gulf crisis in 1990–91 chose to act in an atypically assertive, if not aggressive, manner, one repeated before and during the Yemeni civil war in 1994. Moreover, unlike these instances in the first half of the 1990s, in the near future these rulers may not have the luxury of free choice between this new assertiveness and their more characteristic mode of behavior. They may not have the economic surplus to base external relations so heavily on what some have called 'riyalpolitik' and they may be subjected to such domestic political pressures as to lead them to act on the peninsula in a more adventurous, less farsighted way.[10]

Undoing the Negative Effects

What can the UAE and the other Arab Gulf states do to counter the negative effects of the Yemeni civil war of 1994? If they want to restore the emergent, barely evident balance-of-power system that afforded them some protection from an overbearing Saudi Arabia before the Gulf crisis, then they must re-establish reasonably good working relations with Yemen. Such relations are a necessary condition for the restoration of a capacity to make and unmake coalitions easily—i.e. to strike new power balances under new conditions and in new situations. Simply put, Yemen must be restored to the status of potential ally in the game of nations on the peninsula.

The likely formula to normalize relations quickly involves a *quid pro quo* in which each side asks the other to forgive and forget. Yemen would forgive and forget the support given to the South by the UAE and other Arab Gulf states; for their part, these states would do the same regarding Yemen's failure to support the Saudi- and US-led coalition during the Gulf crisis. Given the new symmetry of wrongs, there is no reason why either side should have to come to the other on its knees and beg forgiveness—it can and should be a dignified, mutually beneficial act of reconciliation. Moreover, it is a possible step, and a small one at that. Yemen indicated an eagerness to open a new chapter on relations with the Arab Gulf states during the weeks immediately after its victory over the South, as it had a year earlier in mid-1993 (and, indeed, since the spring of 1991). For their parts, the UAE and Oman seemed prepared to meet Yemen halfway at this time. By contrast, Kuwait still refused to take this step.

Restored relations between Yemen and the Arab Gulf states is a necessary but not sufficient condition for the revival of a flexible system of countervailing powers. Meeting this condition will not achieve the desired result so long as Yemen and Saudi Arabia are locked in a conflict relationship that ranges only narrowly between cold war and the threat, if not the actual waging, of hot war. Apart from the possibility of a war that would surely impact on other states on the Arabian peninsula, continuous high-level conflict between Yemen and Saudi Arabia would make coalition formation on the peninsula less fluid and more inflexible, thereby constraining and compromising this crude balancing mechanism. Accordingly, in addition to improving their relations with Yemen, the UAE and the other Arab Gulf states should urge an accommodation between the Saudis and the Yemenis. Each can approach both Yemen and Saudi Arabia bilaterally—at the same time that each approaches the Saudis through the institutions of the GCC.

The capacity of the other Arab Gulf states to help meet this second condition for a system of balances—i.e. the normalization of relations between Yemen and Saudi Arabia—is limited. Between these two next-door neighbors, the conflict issues are real and the grievances are deeply felt. The Saudis truly distrust and fear a united and democratic Yemen; the catastrophic expulsion of the Yemeni workers by the Saudis made the Yemenis and their government angry and resentful; and the border disputes between the two neighbors are substantial and not open to easy resolution. On top of all of this is the new animosity between the Saudis and the Yemenis that was fuelled by the Yemeni civil war of 1994.[11] Clearly, Saudi Arabia and Yemen themselves must deal with these legacies of their past relations. Yemen did state in mid-July 1994, as it has said since 1991, that it wanted to close the old chapter on Saudi-Yemeni relations and to open a new one. The neighboring Arab Gulf states can only try to hold the Yemenis to these words and to persuade them to act accordingly—and to urge the Saudis to respond in kind.

Conclusion

In conclusion, the bloc-like pattern in which the Arab Gulf states are united with Saudi Arabia against Yemen, the pattern forged in the Gulf crisis and reinforced in the Yemeni civil war, probably exposes those states to increased pressure and control by the Saudis. Ironically, the stronger the ties between the Saudis and these neighboring states, the greater the pressure and control of the former over the latter. If these Arab Gulf states are not concerned about this situation, then there is no problem. (If they are not, then no one else in the world is likely to be concerned, except perhaps Yemen.) But if they are concerned, then they should promptly make serious efforts both to normalize their relations with Yemen and to persuade Saudi Arabia to do the same. The goal should be a version, perhaps an improved version, of the open, fluid system that allowed for the easy formation of loose, informal, often fleeting coalitions on the Arabian peninsula in the 1970s and 1980s. A pattern of relations that encourages somewhat opportunistic, situational-based alliances seems best for the peninsula in the last half-decade of the twentieth century, a changing subregion now occupied by five small states and two large ones—Saudi Arabia and Yemen.

Ending Yemen's isolation may do more than lessen the chance that the country will turn to Iraq, Iran or Sudan for support—and serve their regional purposes in the process.[12] The GCC will remain the rather empty and weak collective security vehicle of the Arab Gulf states, and it is unlikely that relations between Saudi Arabia and Yemen will improve in the foreseeable future to the point where the former could bring itself to accord the latter GCC membership or even 'partnership for peace' status.[13] Paradoxically, however, a pattern that allowed for close ties between Yemen and the neighboring Arab Gulf states would make it more possible for those states to enter safely into a closer collective security regimen with their larger Saudi neighbor, a goal which has eluded the GCC and its members since 1981.

CHAPTER FIVE

External Powers and the Yemeni Civil War

Mark N. Katz

The 1994 Yemeni civil war is the seventh occasion that Yemenis have fought among themselves since 1962.[1] This latest conflict, however, is the first to occur outside the Cold War context. For the first time, then, conflict in Yemen is not being perceived, or misperceived, as part of the Soviet-American struggle for influence in the third world that so dominated world politics in the recent past. For no matter what the role of outside powers in Yemen's previous conflicts, all of them had their roots in internal Yemeni quarrels. This latest civil war is no exception. Nevertheless, just as with previous Yemeni conflicts, the 1994 civil war and its aftermath have had important regional implications. And, despite the end of the Cold War, this latest civil war may also have important global dimensions.

The motives and actions (to the extent they are known) of the relevant external powers with regard to the 1994 Yemeni civil war and its aftermath will be discussed here. First to be examined will be the role of those regional powers which supported (more or less actively) the South. The role of the regional powers which backed the unity government based in San'a' will then be analyzed. The role of extra-regional powers will also be looked at. Finally, the chapter will address the broader challenge that the Yemeni civil war and its aftermath pose for the Gulf Cooperation Council (GCC) countries and the West, as well as the policy choices they face in dealing with this situation.

The Yemeni War of 1994: Causes and Consequences

Siding with the South

Saudi Arabia's actions served most to strengthen the South *vis-à-vis* San'a' both during the civil war and afterwards.[2] Saudi efforts to achieve a cease-fire were perceived in San'a' as an effort to aid the South: if a cease-fire had taken hold, the Southern government would have had a greater opportunity to consolidate its independence. Towards the end of the conflict, Saudi Arabia reportedly attempted to persuade other Arab governments to recognize the independence of the South.[3] According to a number of sources, Saudi Arabia also provided military assistance to the Southern forces. This may have included purchasing modern Soviet-built MiG-29 fighter-bombers for the South. According to the International Institute for Strategic Studies, the Yemenis did not possess such aircraft before the war.[4] But Southern forces did employ them during the conflict.[5] Further, even after Northern forces defeated the South, Saudi Arabia has reportedly provided sanctuary to the fleeing Southern leadership and the remnants of its armed forces.[6]

It is ironic that Riyadh would back the former Marxist rulers of South Yemen whom only a few years previously the Saudis had regarded as enemies. There are several reasons, however, why the Saudis opposed the unification of Yemen in 1990 and the regime of 'Ali 'Abdullah Salih, the president of North Yemen from 1978 until unification and the president of united Yemen since then.[7]

First, there are outstanding territorial disputes between Riyadh and San'a'. In 1934 Saudi Arabia and North Yemen fought a brief war in which the former captured 'Asir from the latter. The 1934 Saudi-Yemeni treaty ending the war, however, did not grant 'Asir to the Saudis permanently, but only for a twenty-year renewable term. The treaty was renewed in 1954 and 1974, and was up for renewal again in 1994. In addition, other territorial disputes arose between Saudi Arabia and Yemen where their common borders had never been demarcated. The dispute involved rival claims over territory in the eastern part of former North Yemen and the northern area of former South Yemen where oil companies operating under concessions granted by the Yemenis had either found oil or hoped to do so.

The territorial dispute has been compounded by Yemeni unification. Until unification in 1990, the two Yemens focused their attention primarily on each other. While the two countries were independent, each usually regarded the other as its primary security threat. With the achievement of unity, however, Yemeni foreign policy has focused on disputes with Saudi Arabia. Instead of two smaller nations chronically at odds with each other, Yemeni unity meant that the Saudis found a big country with a population larger than that of their own on their south-western border. Further, with the discovery of significant quantities of oil and the probability that even more might be found, Riyadh faced the prospect of a united Yemen which could use its new-found economic resources to build up its armed forces *vis-à-vis* Saudi Arabia.

The Saudis may also have feared progress towards democratization in Yemen, where a remarkable degree of political freedom did indeed develop. Many independent newspapers appeared which harshly criticized the top leadership of the country. Some even openly called for the resignation of President Salih. The Yemeni parliamentary elections of April 1993 were certified as free and fair by a large number of international observers. *The Economist* termed this 'the Arab world's most democratic election'.[8] Of course, united Yemen could hardly be called a full-fledged democracy; the degree of control exercised by President Salih, without reference either to the parliament or the Southern members of the five-man Presidential Council which he chairs, was an important cause of the civil war. Nevertheless some observers noted that the Saudi leadership regarded democratization in Yemen as highly threatening since it might serve to fuel demands for political change in the Kingdom of Saudi Arabia itself.

The most important reason why the Saudis came to oppose the regime of Salih in particular is San'a''s stance during the 1990-91 Gulf war. While San'a' has since claimed that it was neutral and only sought to help resolve the conflict peacefully, its actions at the time definitely aided Iraq. The Yemeni call for an 'Arab solution' to the crisis greatly angered the Saudis since those Arab states which opposed Saddam's invasion of Kuwait were not capable of dislodging his forces by themselves or of defending Saudi Arabia from a subsequent Iraqi attack. The Saudis were especially bitter about San'a''s conduct after Riyadh had provided large-scale economic assistance to Salih's government. The argument that Salih's pro-Iraqi stance reflected Yemeni public opinion only increased Saudi concerns that democratization in Yemen was threatening to Saudi rule.

Saudi support for the South in the 1994 Yemeni civil war could have had, if the Southerners had been successful, several positive benefits from Riyadh's point of view. First, the rebirth of South Yemen would have meant a return to what was for the Saudis the more congenial situation of two smaller Yemens focusing their efforts on each other rather than one large Yemen focusing on its border dispute with Saudi Arabia. Second, a state of war or tension in Yemen would probably have led to a halt to democratization in the country and, hence, to whatever threat this may have posed to Saudi internal stability. Third, the loss of South Yemen would have, at minimum, greatly weakened Salih's position. At maximum, the Saudis may have calculated that his failure to prevent the South from seceding might even have led to his overthrow.

Saudi Arabia was the regional power with the greatest incentive to support the South, but it was not the only such state to do so. Kuwait also reportedly gave financial assistance to the Southern cause. Towards the end of the conflict, the Kuwaiti foreign minister openly talked about granting diplomatic recognition to the South.[9] Kuwait, obviously, does not have a border dispute with Yemen. Nor is it particularly concerned with progress towards democratization there as Kuwait also enjoys a relatively free press and, for some of its citizens, relatively free elections for its parliament. Nor did Yemeni unity *per se* pose any particular threat to Kuwait.

The primary motivation for Kuwait to support the South was continuing Kuwaiti anger over President Salih's support for Saddam Hussein during Iraq's occupation of Kuwait after years of Kuwaiti economic assistance to Yemen. For this, the Kuwaitis too would like to have seen Salih punished, weakened and possibly overthrown.[10]

Other nations took actions—or San'a' perceived that they took actions—which supported the South. The UAE, Oman, Bahrain, Egypt and Syria all more or less strongly supported a cease-fire in the Yemeni civil war. If a cease-fire had been put into effect, this might have helped the Southerners consolidate their regime. To a lesser extent than Saudi Arabia, Oman reportedly provided refuge to some of the Southern leadership and armed forces fleeing South Yemen at the end of the conflict.[11] The governments of these states do not have the visceral dislike for President Salih that the leaders of Saudi Arabia and Kuwait feel. Their motives for supporting the South appear to be twofold:

(i) a general desire to weaken a pro-Iraqi government, which Salih's regime is still perceived to be; and

(ii) a desire to reap the rewards of collaboration with Saudi Arabia and Kuwait on an issue that is clearly of great importance to these two governments, although it may be of only minor significance to their allies in the region.

Finally, it should be mentioned that the one government that recognized South Yemen was the, itself, universally unrecognized government of the 'Somaliland Republic' (northern Somalia) which seceded from Somalia. Northern Somaliland's motive appears to have been a desire to recognize (and have recognized) secession as legitimate. Despite the South Yemeni desire to be recognized, the Southern government placed so little value on the Somaliland Republic's act that it did not even bother to recognize it in return.

Siding with the North

There were some governments in the region which reportedly sided with the North, or unity government, during the civil war. One such government was Qatar. Although Qatar played an active role in the UN-sponsored intervention against Iraq, there was a border clash between Qatar and Saudi Arabia in 1992. Relations between them are still poor. Qatar did not join in the call by the other GCC states for a cease-fire in Yemen[12] and, according to some sources, the country provided financial assistance to the Salih government during the conflict.

Jordan was also reported to have backed the Salih government. Like Yemen, Jordan took actions which aided Iraq during the 1990-91 Gulf war. And also like Yemen, Jordan incurred the wrath of Saudi Arabia and Kuwait for doing so. Unlike Yemen, Jordan was able to restore its relations with the US and the West to a considerable extent. Its relations with Saudi Arabia and Kuwait, however, remain strained. Jordan, along with Oman, actively sought to mediate the dispute between 'Ali 'Abdullah Salih and 'Ali Salim al-Bid before the civil war broke out. According to one source, Jordanian air force personnel helped service Yemen's inventory of US F-5s during the civil war.[13]

Another state that sided with the Salih government was Iraq. Baghdad's motive for aiding the Salih regime is obvious: Iraq sought to thwart the possible extension of Saudi influence had the Southern effort succeeded. According to some sources, Iraqi officers helped organize the

North's military campaign against the South.[14] Whether these reports are accurate or not, it is clear that Iraq was not in a position to aid San'a' as much as it could have done if the UN sanctions against Baghdad had been lifted.

Sudan also sided with San'a'. The leadership of this country's Muslim fundamentalist regime has close ties with Shaykh 'Abd al-Majid al-Zindani, one of the top leaders of the Yemeni Reform Grouping (YRG or Islah) in Yemen. During the conflict, the YRG sided with President Salih and condemned Saudi support for the South. Yet while the Sudanese may have given full political support to San'a', they were not in a position to provide much in terms of material support due to the civil war with their own Southern secessionists as well as the country's general poverty. Sudan merely acknowledged sending 'assistance' to Yemen at the end of the war.[15]

Colonel Qadhdhafi of Libya, who often pursues an anti-Saudi policy, was also said to have supported San'a'. It is doubtful, however, that he provided much material support to the Salih government.[16] Iran was also reported to have backed the Northern cause. Iran has had a long-standing rivalry with Saudi Arabia, and thus would not want to see Saudi influence in Yemen extended. Nevertheless, Iran is currently attempting to build a *rapprochement* with Saudi Arabia.[17] To the extent that any Iranian assistance went to San'a', it is said to have gone indirectly— perhaps through Sudan.[18]

Informed observers in Washington claim that the amount of external assistance received by the North during the 1994 civil war was minuscule compared to that received by the South. Politically, however, the Arab world sided with the North by refusing to heed Saudi and Kuwaiti calls for the diplomatic recognition of the South. Despite their aid to the South, Saudi Arabia and Kuwait themselves did not take this step.

External Powers

United States foreign policy has traditionally regarded Yemen as something less than a high priority. The importance of the Yemens was seen mainly in terms of the Cold War competition with the USSR, in addition to how developments there affected neighboring Saudi Arabia —whose security the US has long considered vital to its interests.

Although US Cold War concerns about Yemen are now gone, Washington remains concerned at how events in Yemen affect Saudi Arabia. In the past, Washington has usually followed Riyadh's lead in terms of policy towards the Yemens. But US interest in Yemen has not been exclusively related to Saudi Arabia, especially since an American corporation—Hunt Oil Co.—discovered oil in North Yemen in 1984 and has operated a concession there (in partnership with Exxon) since then. The Canadian subsidiary of an American firm, Occidental, is involved in the extraction of oil from former South Yemen. A number of oil companies from the US and other countries have been exploring for oil elsewhere in Yemen. In addition, Yemen's democratization efforts in recent years, especially the 1993 parliamentary elections, were actively supported by the growing 'democracy lobby': the National Endowment for Democracy, the US Agency for International Development and the organizations they fund.[19]

During the Yemeni civil war, the United States supported the efforts by the GCC (with the exception of Qatar) to arrange for a cease-fire at the UN. Knowledgeable US government officials attributed most of the cease-fire violations to the North and reportedly issued strong protests to officials from San'a'. The US, however, did not take any practical measures either to enforce a cease-fire or to impose sanctions for violating it. The US had also supported Yemeni unity when it occurred in 1990. Washington has taken a rather poor view of secession attempts ever since the American civil war, and was not willing to recognize South Yemen as Riyadh and Kuwait urged.[20]

The policy of the other Western powers was basically the same as that of the US. Some speculated that Russia might support its old allies in the South, but there appears to be no evidence that this occurred and Russia launched a diplomatic effort to resolve the conflict. The Russian foreign ministry hoped that Moscow's previously close relationship with both the Northern and Southern leaderships would put Moscow in a better position than others to successfully mediate between the opposing sides: it did not.

Russia did not necessarily have a particular stake in the war ending one way or another. Its mediation attempt was part of Moscow's larger effort to have Russia accepted as a great power by the rest of the world. Russia, however, may have sold the MiG-29s to the Saudis for retransfer to the South. If so, the Russian defence ministry's motive is more likely to have been commercial than political: it needed hard currency. The aircraft, however, may have come from Eastern Europe, North Korea or some other country possessing such weapons and also in need of hard currency.

It appears that no extra-regional power deliberately gave any direct material assistance to either the North or the South during the conflict. Like the Arab nations, however, the rest of the world gave political support to the Northern cause by not extending diplomatic recognition to the South.

Future Implications and Choices

The Southern effort has been defeated and Yemen remains united under the rule of President Salih. Further, San'a' triumphed with minimal external assistance. Despite the significant external support that the Southern leadership reportedly received from Saudi Arabia, Kuwait and other GCC states, it was driven out of Yemen altogether. What are the implications stemming from how the Yemeni civil war ended? The most obvious concerns Yemen itself: President Salih is firmly in control of the country, at least at present. But the outcome of the civil war has ramifications that extend beyond Yemen.

The first of these is the further worsening of relations between the Salih government on the one hand and most of the GCC states—especially Saudi Arabia—on the other. Because of Saudi aid to the South, San'a' more than ever regards Riyadh as its implacable enemy. The fact that Riyadh has taken in the bulk of the Southern forces who managed to flee Yemen at the end of the war has, understandably, convinced the Salih government that the Saudis may well attempt to undermine it again. The Saudis, for their part, are hardly likely to feel friendlier to Salih after their attempt to aid his opponents failed.

Yemen's relations with the other GCC states (except Qatar) are also poor, but not to the same extent as its relations with the Kingdom of Saudi Arabia, for it is Saudi Arabia which presents the greatest threat to the Salih government. If Saudi policy towards San'a' suddenly became friendly and accommodating, it is highly doubtful that the other GCC states would or could continue a hostile policy towards Yemen. But even if the other GCC states improved their relations with Yemen (as Oman and the UAE are reportedly doing), this would probably do little to abate Saudi-Yemeni hostility.[21]

Whereas increased Saudi-Yemeni hostility is likely to be one long-term result of the 1994 Yemeni civil war, there is another which is more disturbing. Tension between Yemen on the one hand and Saudi Arabia and the GCC on the other does not exist in a void. The states of the Arabian peninsula face other active or potential enemies. These include Iraq, Iran, Sudan and the Islamic revolutionary movements that are attempting to seize power in Egypt, Algeria and other Middle Eastern countries. Although it is very difficult to obtain reliable information, Saudi Arabia itself faces some degree of internal opposition, including that from Islamic revolutionaries.[22]

So long as Saudi-Yemeni tension continues, it will be possible for Saudi Arabia's other opponents to take advantage of this tension by supporting Yemen. The 1994 Yemeni civil war took place at a time when the actual and potential opponents of Saudi Arabia and the GCC states were relatively weak or not strongly involved, but this situation may not last.

Although the UN embargo against Iraq has held relatively firm up to the present, there are several countries with a strong interest in seeing it ended, including Turkey, Russia, China and France. Their motivation is primarily financial. If and when Iraq is able to resume exporting oil, it will have an important source of revenue which could be used not only for rebuilding its military, but also for aiding the enemies of its enemies—namely Yemen.

Iran is now pursuing something akin to *détente* with Saudi Arabia. But *détente* is not love. The Iranian revolutionary ethos is fundamentally opposed to all monarchies. If Islamic revolutionary forces grew stronger in other Muslim countries, it is highly unlikely that Tehran would abstain from supporting them for the sake of good relations with Riyadh. Providing support for Yemen is always an option for Tehran if Saudi-Iranian relations turn sour again.

If Islamic revolutionary regimes come to power elsewhere in the Arab world, they are likely to be highly anti-Western as well as virulently opposed to any Arab government they identify as being allied with the West, such as those in Saudi Arabia and the rest of the GCC. It is when revolutionary regimes first come to power that they usually attempt to export their revolution. Continuing Saudi-Yemeni tension would offer them an opportunity to exploit as well.

Finally, if any serious form of opposition arose, or was perceived to arise, within Saudi Arabia, the country's enemies would not hesitate to try to support it. If Saudi Arabia continues to accommodate San'a''s opponents on Saudi territory, Yemen can be expected to accommodate Saudi Arabia's opponents on its—from which they could more easily receive assistance from Riyadh's other enemies. The problem with the continuation of bitterly hostile relations between San'a' and Riyadh is that the Saudis' other enemies can exploit this hostility by supporting Yemen against Saudi Arabia. At minimum, their support could serve to thwart the achievement of Saudi aims with regard to Yemen. At maximum, an alliance between Yemen and one or more of the Kingdom of Saudi Arabia's other enemies could pose a security threat to Saudi Arabia and the rest of the GCC.

The policy question that arises for Saudi Arabia and the GCC, as well as their allies in the West and elsewhere, is how Saudi-Yemeni tension can be de-linked from the GCC's other opponents, actual or potential. It is probably not possible to de-link these two problems if Saudi-Yemeni tension continues. For, as was noted before, so long as this tension continues, it can be exploited by others. The only way to prevent it, then, is somehow to bring an end to Saudi-Yemeni tension so that it no longer exists for others to take advantage of.

There are basically only two ways to do this: either through pursuing a very 'hard' policy towards Yemen or through pursuing a very 'soft' one. The first option has an obvious appeal for Saudi Arabia and some other GCC states. If Salih could be overthrown and replaced by a regime friendlier to the GCC, or if Yemen could be divided, with a government dependent on the GCC in the South and the Salih regime at best struggling to survive in the North, Saudi Arabia and the GCC could eliminate, or at least greatly diminish, their Yemen problem.

The difficulty with pursuing such a policy is that it is very difficult to implement successfully. Since the time of the Gulf war, Saudi Arabia, in particular, has pursued a hard policy towards Yemen, but it has failed. This is because the Saudis have consistently miscalculated the effect of their policies on their neighbor. By expelling some 800,000 Yemeni workers from the Kingdom of Saudi Arabia in retaliation for Salih's pro-Iraqi stance during the Gulf war, the Saudis turned what had been their dispute with the Salih government into a dispute with the entire Yemeni nation. If the Saudi leaders believed that the expelled Yemenis and the families who depended on their remittances would work to overthrow Salih in order to restore Yemen to Riyadh's good graces, they were grossly mistaken. Instead, the incident merely served to intensify popular Yemeni hatred for the Saudis.

Similarly, supporting the South in the 1994 civil war was a major miscalculation. It is true that despite the holding of parliamentary elections in 1993 and the emergence of a relatively free press, President Salih's rule has been something less than democratic. It is also true that many Southerners were resentful that Northerners had come to dominate the unified government and that the economic situation in the South had become especially difficult. But even if many Southerners had become disillusioned with Salih's rule, this did not mean they were prepared to support the former Marxist leadership who had run South Yemen dictatorially in the past and were deeply unpopular there. Indeed, the Southern leadership itself remains sharply divided because of, among many other episodes, the 1986 South Yemeni civil war in which the socialists fought a bitter war with each other.

Further, opposition to Salih's rule did not equate with opposition to unity. During the civil war, delegations from several Yemeni groups came to Washington. While many of them—including some from Salih's own General People's Congress (GPC)—expressed opposition to Salih, they were adamant about the maintenance of Yemeni unity. Because those fighting against Salih sought secession, and the South was known to receive Saudi backing, they lost the support of Yemeni nationalists.

The Saudis may be about to miscalculate again if they think that they can weaken Salih through supporting the Southern forces which fled from Yemen at the end of the war. If these forces could not succeed in establishing Southern independence while they were inside the country, they are even less likely to be able to do so now that they are outside it. Further, the Saudis do not seem to understand that it is their sponsorship of the South that serves to discredit them among Yemeni nationalists.

It is possible, of course, that if San'a' imposes harsh rule now that the civil war is over, opposition to the regime will rise again. But neither the Saudis nor anyone else can assume that a popular Yemeni opposition force challenging Salih will in any way be pro-Saudi. The most important force that allied with Salih to defeat the South was the YRG. This may have surprised the Saudis, who regarded one of the YRG's main leaders, Shaykh 'Abdullah al-Ahmar of Hashid, as their friend. Al-Ahmar, however, may well have condemned Saudi support for the South and sided with Salih for fear that if he did not, he would lose control of the YRG to the radical Shaykh 'Abd al-Majid al-Zindani, who has close links to the Islamic fundamentalist government in Sudan. If opposition to Salih's rule does grow, we may witness a struggle between a pro-Iraqi Salih and a pro-Sudanese/pro-Iranian YRG. In other words, no one can assume that the demise of Salih will bring to power in San'a' a government that is friendlier to Saudi Arabia.

In contrast with a hard policy, a soft policy towards Yemen would recognize: first, that Yemeni unity is here to stay; and second, that Salih's regime may well remain in power, but even if it does not, it is unlikely to be replaced by a pro-Saudi government. A soft policy, then, would seek to de-link Yemen from the GCC's other regional opponents by establishing peaceful coexistence with San'a'. Such a policy would end all support to San'a''s political opponents, especially those which seek to end Yemeni unity. This policy would also include allowing Yemeni workers to return to Saudi Arabia and other Gulf countries as well as resuming economic assistance.

Some might object that Saudi Arabia and the GCC have pursued a soft policy towards Yemen in the past and were rewarded with Yemeni support for Iraq after its invasion of Kuwait. But many Yemenis recognized—both then and now—that San'a''s position in the Gulf war cost Yemen dearly. There is evidence that President Salih himself acknowledges this. At the very moment of his triumph over the South, he sent a message to King Fahd calling for 'good-neighborly relations and cooperation' between Saudi Arabia and Yemen.[23] At the very least, allowing the traditional pattern of economic relations between Yemen and the GCC to resume can start the process of reducing the Yemeni popular animosity against Saudi Arabia that Salih has been able to exploit so effectively.

In the final analysis, the GCC's 'Yemen problem' may not be one that can be resolved, but only managed. For even if the GCC pursued a soft policy towards Yemen by resuming aid and normal economic relations, San'a' would undoubtedly accept aid from the GCC's opponents if it were offered. This is a game that Salih played to brilliant effect during his presidency of North Yemen during the Cold War when he received assistance from the USSR on the one hand and the GCC as well as the US on the other. But it was also a game that Saudi Arabia and the other GCC states played successfully too. Although Riyadh did not have complete influence in San'a', it made sure that no one else did either. From 1990 until now, the hard policy towards Yemen has failed. Just as in the past with North Yemen, however, the soft policy option is a game that Saudi Arabia and the GCC are in a strong position to play successfully with united Yemen.

Conclusion

Jamal S. al-Suwaidi

The preceding chapters have brought out several themes that inform the debate over the causes and consequences of the 1994 Yemeni civil war. Understudied and overshadowed by strategic concerns over Gulf security and the stability of the Arab Gulf states, the situation in Yemen has received neither the public nor the scholarly attention commensurate with its historical and geographic place in the Arabian peninsula. As a result, regional reverberations associated with political turmoil in the Yemens are often misunderstood, with potentially damaging effects on the security and prosperity of the region.

No single theme readily captures the turbulent events that transpired during the Yemen conflict, though some appear to have eclipsed others in their saliency. The conflict was at once a dispute over power-sharing at the top, about the equitable distribution of wealth, about the exigency of political pluralism, and, not least, about differing visions of nation-state building in the post-Cold War era. If these are the principal themes that characterized the conflict internally, externally the conflict was driven largely by Yemen's precarious relationship with Saudi Arabia, by Yemen's political isolation from the GCC in the wake of the 1990–91 Gulf war, by the absence of any extra-regional power to contain the warring parties, and by the lack of unity among regional states, particularly GCC members, to bring about a peaceful resolution.

Yemen's most recent civil war was, first and foremost, a struggle between two personalities whose differences were not reflected in people

Conclusion

beyond those closely identified with the leadership and military of both North and South Yemen. With a marginal role played by tribes, and Cold War-type outside manipulation all but vanished, the ambitions of a few—namely, 'Ali 'Abdullah Salih and 'Ali Salim al-Bid—generated the calamity of the many. Unwilling to relinquish their respective power bases, leaders in both North and South Yemen entered a compact without the requisite commitment. Unity in 1990 was declared before the planned referendum on the country's constitution, while both sides failed to fully merge key institutions, most notably the military. Economically, this meant massive inefficiencies and duplication in the public sector, an inability to attract foreign investment, and the disproportionate allocation of resources for military and government security forces. The attendant rise in corruption and poverty, exacerbated by the sudden return of some 800,000 Yemeni expatriates no longer welcome in Saudi Arabia, helped fuel public discontent and extremism. Unable to enforce import controls and tariffs and to stem the unofficial currency market, the authorities were faced with a crippled economy and a fragmented government.

Clearly, President Salih's chances of keeping the country reunited will depend in large measure on his ability to put the economy back on track in order to meet the social and economic needs of the country and, second, to achieve political reconciliation between North and South in order to restart the process of political integration. This requires the reconstitution of a multi-party coalition to form a government that is sufficiently inclusive to reflect the diverse political landscape of a united Yemen. A repressive, more parochial and isolationist political climate will not only stifle foreign investment, without which economic growth is scarcely possible, but it will also open up the opportunity for extremist factions to find a receptive audience.

To continue his authoritarian rule while permitting a measure of liberalization, President Salih will have to walk a political tightrope that will test his skills to manage opposition forces at home and to conduct a balanced foreign policy abroad. Relations with Saudi Arabia will continue to set the tone, as the 'Asir, Najran and Jizan areas are still a sensitive issue for the Yemeni people. Hence, the Ta'if Treaty of 1934, which stipulated Saudi sovereignty over the three areas, remains a source of serious tension, since the San'a' government is not prepared publicly to recognize the northern border as final and permanent. Potential oil

Conclusion

deposits in that area compound the issue, as the Saudi authorities have warned companies prospecting there not to infringe on the country's territory. Recent clashes around the town of al-Buqa and rounds of unsuccessful border negotiations are a stark reminder of how serious and seemingly intractable the two sides are. Wrangling over territory may escalate beyond the three provinces. The remaining 1,000 miles of border between Yemen and Saudi Arabia have never been precisely established. Located along the fringes of the desolate Empty Quarter, territorial demarcation of this area is likely to be complicated by Yemen's discovery of oil nearby and uncertainty about the loyalty of tribal inhabitants. Bilateral relations could be further rocked by San'a''s perception of Riyadh's strategic ambitions. Hemmed in by the Suez Canal and the Bab al-Mandab on the Red Sea and the Strait of Hormuz on the Gulf, Saudi Arabia may feel compelled to seek an opening through Yemen to secure its oil exports, after a proposal for a corridor crossing Oman fell on deaf ears.

Similarly, San'a''s complaints over Saudi support of the South and assistance to tribal groupings in the North can scarcely be ignored. President Salih's determination to consolidate his political power is likely to be challenged by both moderate Southern leaders intent on seeking greater influence in return for their wartime allegiance, as well as members of Islah who are trying to cash in for their support against the 'atheist' South. Assistance to either faction will almost certainly be regarded as Saudi meddling in the internal affairs of its neighbor. Attempts at destabilizing the Salih regime may not readily subside, given the lingering effect of San'a''s stance during the 1990–91 Gulf war. Yemen's ambivalence in the face of global condemnation of Iraqi aggression against Kuwait greatly harmed the chance for more harmonious relations between San'a' and its neighbors. Salih's call for an 'Arab solution' and his subsequent reliance on Iraqi technical assistance for the military, including the establishment of a revolutionary guard modeled after Saddam Hussein's, were of no reassurance to the Saudis, who had hoped for Yemen's support during the Gulf crisis. The UAE and Kuwait felt especially slighted by Salih's actions, after having spent millions of dollars to assist in the economic development of Yemen. Hence, the punishment meted out by Riyadh is unlikely to abate should Yemeni leaders fail to project some sensitivity on the issue. Further fence-sitting in times of outside aggression against peninsula neighbors will merely fuel the country's

Conclusion

political isolation from the other GCC members, whose support it will need in order to allay Saudi fears of a politically reinvigorated, demographically superior and, perhaps, economically thriving united Yemen. Having to contend with restive Iraq and Iran in the north, Riyadh has compelling reasons to contain its enemies and obviate the specter of being pressured on two sides.

To defuse bilateral tensions with Saudi Arabia and prevent further domestic instability, the San'a' government must pursue true integration, not just amalgamation, of North and South. Holding the upper hand, President Salih has the opportunity to extend the superior bureaucratic and organizational structure of the South to the rest of the country, while holding out the benefits of economic growth, based on the combined resources of North and South, to all Yemenis. Economic diversification away from an over-dependence on oil (which currently generates 85% of export earnings) and an emphasis on the export development of agriculture, fishing and mineral resources, coupled with the development of Aden as a free port, are the keys to long-term prosperity.[1] This will help Yemen become an attractive locale for foreign investment—rather than foreign aid—from Arab neighbors and the West.

The importance of Yemen's economic well-being is difficult to overstate. With a fertility rate estimated at 7.5%, more than twice the world average, Yemen's population is expected to grow by 3.4% per annum and may reach 16.5 million by the year 2000. Coupled with an adult literacy rate of only 41%, the challenge facing the country is formidable but not insurmountable.[2] To compensate for virtually stagnant oil production, Yemen is seeking to exploit an estimated 20-30 million cubic feet of gas, an effort which will rest on the government's ability to reassure outside investors and energy companies bidding for contracts. Equally critical is the reduction of the massive budget deficit which has strangled attempts at economic recovery. Cutting government subsidies and state employment, without which a recovery is scarcely possible, may seriously undercut President Salih's popularity. There are ominous signs the economy will contract by 10% over the next two years and suffer a dramatic rise in inflation.[3] To steer clear of financial collapse and further economic deprivation, the government must devote itself quickly to the reconstruction of the war-torn country and the smoothing of relations with its Gulf neighbors. Without rearranging budget priorities, whereby military spending is drastically curtailed in

Conclusion

favor of public health and education, potential outside donors are unlikely to be forthcoming in their assistance. It is upon the Salih government to reassure those willing to aid, that their investments are properly spent. To this end, a *modus vivendi* with the Saudis on the principal issues of borders, Islamic radicalism, and labor migration is indispensable. Similarly, a participatory government that allows for the representation and *integration* of the former South Yemen is a necessary step for the Salih regime in order to scale back military expenditures in favor of infrastructure development and social programs such as education and medical care. A united Yemen that is reconciled internally and on its way to economic recovery is also more likely to join the GCC community.

The challenge of national unity is of no small order. A unified Yemen faces a host of difficult socio-economic problems that range from illiteracy to lack of adequate medical services and schools, and from mounting poverty to the inequitable distribution of wealth associated with the disproportionate ownership of productive assets by a minority of rulers, tribal chiefs, and leading officials. Although the internal divisions that led to civil strife may continue to complicate efforts to rebuild national unity, the recently concluded conflict is giving the Salih government a fresh chance to reunite the Yemeni people without committing the mistakes that helped doom the previous attempt at unification. A government offer to extend an amnesty to former members of the Southern leadership is a welcome gesture; the Salih regime should be held to it by the international community to ensure true national reconciliation. The recent return of thousands of Yemeni refugees who fled the civil war is reassuring in that regard. Conversely, Salih's overtures to Gulf leaders, including a message to King Fahd of Saudi Arabia expressing 'eagerness to turn over a new leaf in Yemeni-Saudi relations', should serve as a beginning for a GCC *rapprochement* with San'a'.[4]

The study of political change in Yemen illustrates the major problems that developing countries face after the end of the Cold War. Yemen is confronted with a number of questions that will test the leadership's political acumen to navigate the country away from the divisive issues towards national stability governed by mutual interest in both North and South for common prosperity. The latter is achievable only through a policy that carefully combines the need for national reconciliation with the exigency of amicable foreign relations. Whether

Conclusion

the Salih leadership will succeed in this task will hinge largely on its ability to put the economy back on track. Austerity measures appear unavoidable in the short run in order to instill confidence in the international financial community that Yemen has the potential to become an attractive investment. To do so, the country will have to adopt an economic model that suits the dynamics of social interaction of Yemeni society. It should promote investment for the long-term development of national resources, including the judicious extraction and export of hydrocarbons and other minerals, in conjunction with the corresponding training of the requisite indigenous labor, to permit economic diversification into downstream industries. Given the paucity of domestic funds and the lack of a skilled labor pool, Yemen's economic future will crucially hinge on the dual task of attracting aid from abroad while pushing ahead with the development of an educated labor force equipped to meet the challenges of operating in a global market. To accomplish both objectives, the Salih government must strive for cordial relations with its Arab neighbors, especially the GCC members who are likely to continue to be the principal source of outside assistance. Hence, a moderate foreign policy that eschews the pitfalls of siding with decidedly destabilizing regimes and political factions is paramount to Yemen's regional rehabilitation. Similarly, the San'a' government's domestic agenda must be anchored in a policy of national reconciliation that ensures due representation of people in both the North and the South. The outcome of the 1994 war should not obscure the great difficulties which Yemen still confronts. Although President Salih has prevailed on the battlefield, he faces a range of daunting problems, none of which are amenable to quick fixes. On the contrary, the stewardship of a united Yemen is likely to test the mettle of the most seasoned politician. The coming years will show whether President Salih will emerge as the architect of a lasting unity and deserving of the patina of a true statesman, or whether he will preside over a fragmented polity perpetuating the social and economic instability that Yemen and the region can ill afford.

Contributors

Jamal S. al-Suwaidi is the Director of the Emirates Center for Strategic Studies and Research in Abu Dhabi, and teaches at the UAE University in Al Ain. Dr. al-Suwaidi has taught courses in political methodology, political culture, comparative government and international relations at the UAE University and also at the University of Wisconsin-Milwaukee. His Ph.D. dissertation, based on opinion surveys among Kuwaitis, Egyptians, and Palestinians in Kuwait, is a comparative study of relationships between political culture and Islam. He is the author of numerous scholarly articles on such subjects as women and development, women and religion, UAE public opinion on the Gulf crisis, democratic perceptions in Arab and Western societies as well as many others. Dr. al-Suwaidi's latest publication is a chapter entitled 'Arab and Western Conceptions of Democracy' in *Democracy, War and Peace in the Middle East*.

Michael C. Hudson is professor of international relations and government and Seif Ghobash professor of Arab studies in the School of Foreign Service at Georgetown University. He holds a Ph.D. in political science from Yale University. His research interests include processes of political liberalization, politics in divided societies, Middle East regional security, US Middle East policy and the Arab-Israeli conflict. He has held Guggenheim and Ford Foundation fellowships and is a past president of the Middle East Studies Association. Among Dr. Hudson's publications are *The Precarious Republic: Political Modernization in Lebanon, Arab Politics: The Search for Legitimacy* and an edited volume, *The Palestinians: New Directions*. He is also the author of numerous scholarly articles and is currently writing a book on political participation in the Middle East.

Paul K. Dresch is a lecturer in social anthropology at the University of Oxford and a fellow of St. John's College. He received his Ph.D. from the University of Oxford and is an expert on the tribes of Yemen. Dr.

Contributors

Dresch is the author of *Tribes, Government and History in Yemen* as well as many scholarly articles in leading professional journals. He has visited Yemen frequently over the past twenty years.

Charles F. Dunbar is president of the Cleveland Council on World Affairs and former US ambassador to Yemen (1988–91). He is a graduate of Harvard College and holds a Masters degree in international affairs from Columbia University. Ambassador Dunbar joined the US Foreign Service in 1962 and served twenty years in a variety of posts in the Middle East including Iran, Afghanistan, North Africa and the Arabian peninsula. He also served as ambassador to Qatar (1983–85). Ambassador Dunbar has contributed scholarly articles to edited volumes and to *The Middle East Journal* and *Asian Survey*, among others.

Robert D. Burrowes is a research scholar at the Middle East Center, University of Washington in Seattle. He holds a Ph.D. in political science from Princeton University. Dr. Burrowes has taught political science at the City University of New York, New York University and the American University of Beirut. His professional experience also includes work with organizations concerned with training and development work in Yemen. He is the author of *The Yemen Arab Republic: The Politics of Development, 1962–1986* and two forthcoming volumes, *The Republic of Yemen: Oil and Unification* and *The Republic of Yemen: An Historical Dictionary*. In addition, Dr. Burrowes has written and published extensively on Middle Eastern topics in leading professional journals.

Mark N. Katz is associate professor of government and politics at George Mason University in Fairfax, Virginia, and senior staff member at the George Mason University International Institute. Dr. Katz received his Ph.D. in political science from the Massachusetts Institute of Technology in 1982. He has been awarded fellowships by the Brookings Institution, the Earhart Foundation, the Kennan Institute for Advanced Russian Studies, the Rockefeller Foundation and the United States Institute of Peace. He is the author of three books and has edited two others on Soviet foreign and military policy. Dr. Katz has also written many articles on the international relations of the former USSR and of the Middle East.

Notes

Chapter 1
1. Pierre Rondot, *Les Institutions Politiques du Liban* (Paris, n.p., 1947).
2. See, e.g., Michael C. Hudson, 'After the Gulf War: Prospects for Democratization in the Arab World', *Middle East Journal* 45:3 (Summer 1991), pp. 407–26.
3. Karl Deutsch et al., *Political Community and the North Atlantic Area* (Princeton, N.J., Princeton University Press, 1957), pp. 5–9.
4. 'Ali Salim al-Bid was the former South Yemeni leader who became vice-president of united Yemen in 1990, then became head of the secessionist government in 1994.
5. Eric Watkins, 'Opening the Way', *Middle East International* no. 412, November 8, 1991.
6. The accused were 'Ali 'Abdullah al-Ahmar (chairman of the Presidential Council), 'Abdullah bin Husayn al-Ahmar (president of the Chamber of Deputies), 'Abd al-Majid al-Zindani (member of the Presidential Council), 'Ali Muhsin al-Ahmar (brigade commander), 'Abd al-Malik al-Siyani (chief-of-staff), Muhammad Salih al-Ahmar, Muhammad 'Abdullah Salih al-Ahmar, Muhammad Isma'il al-Sinhani, 'Abdullah al-Qadi al-Sinhani, 'Ali Salih al-Ahmar, Muhammad Yahya al-Muwari (chief of military police), 'Abd al-Karim al-Iryani (minister of planning), 'Abdullah al-Ashtal (permanent representative to the United Nations), 'Ali al-Siyani (head of military intelligence), 'Abd al-Wahhab al-'Ansi (deputy prime minister) and 'Abd al-Wahhab al-Daylami (president of the Judicial Council). See *al-Hayat* (London), July 4, 1994, p. 1. Note, however, that Shaykh 'Abdullah bin Husayn al-Ahmar is not a relative of President 'Ali 'Abdullah Salih and his al-Ahmar kinsmen.
7. *Middle East International* no. 463, November 19, 1993.
8. Sheila Carapico, 'Elections and Mass Politics in Yemen', *Middle East Report* 23:6 (no. 185, November–December 1993), pp. 2–6, and 'From Ballot Box to Battlefield: The War of the Two 'Alis', *Middle East Report* 25:1 (no. 190, September–October 1994), p. 27.

Additional References
Burrowes, Robert D., 'Prelude to Unification: The Yemen Arab Republic, 1962–90', *International Journal of Middle East Studies* 23:4 (November 1991),

Notes

pp. 483–506.
Democratic Republic of Yemen, Office of the Council of Ministers, 'Verbal Note', *al-Makallah*, June 12, 1994.
Detalle, Renaud, 'The Yemeni Elections Up Close', *Middle East Report* 23:6 (no. 185, November–December 1993), pp. 8–12.
Dunbar, Charles, 'The Unification of Yemen: Process, Politics, and Prospects', *Middle East Journal* 46:3 (Summer 1992), pp. 456–76.
Middle East Watch, 'Yemen: Steps toward Civil Society', *Middle East Watch* 4:10 (November 1992).
Myles, John, 'Yemen's Growing Pains', *Middle East International* no. 438, November 20, 1992.
Warburton, David, 'The War in Yemen', unpublished paper, San'a', June 1994.
Watkins, Eric, and Patrick Makin, 'Yemen's Crisis Threatens the Country's Unity', *Middle East International* no. 463, November 19, 1993.
Watkins, Eric, 'Yemen's Riots Prompt Talk of Reform', *Middle East International* no. 444, February 19, 1993, p. 18.
Whittaker, Brian, 'Up to the Brink', *Middle East International* no. 461, October 22, 1993.
'Yemeni Unification: At Last they Tied the Knot', *The Middle East* no. 189, July 1990, pp. 5–11.

Interviews
Al-'Attas, Haydar Abu Bakr, interview in San'a', June 11, 1990, and in Washington, June 23, 1994.
Nu'man, Yasin Sa'id, interview in San'a', June 11, 1990.
'Umar, Jarallah, interview in San'a', June 6, 1990.
Senior officials of the San'a' government loyal to President 'Ali 'Abdullah Salih, in Washington and San'a', March–August 1994.

Chapter 2
1. My political science colleagues at the ECSSR symposium quoted ambassadors, ministers and even presidents. I have known Yemen long enough to know some prominent people there; but I should stress that most of what follows comes from talking to very ordinary Yemeni citizens. The complementarity of viewpoints may be useful.

    On the unfortunate results of dividing material among different academic subjects see Jeanne Favret, 'Traditionalism through Ultra-modernism', in E. Gellner and C. Michaud (eds), *Arabs and Berbers* (London, Duckworth, 1973), pp. 307–24 (French original 1967).

    The British Academy kindly funded visits to Yemen in 1990 and 1992. The views I express are my own and do not reflect those of any institution.
2. Tribesmen were prominent in regular army units. Regrettably, tribesmen

Notes

unattached to such units, or attached only loosely, took part in looting. But nowhere could one say, 'The Bani Fulan fought on this side or that.'

3. This too will be forgotten, but people in parts of the South, speaking of pre-unity days long before the crisis, said they thought before unity that the Southern leadership would 'go like Nicolae went', meaning Nicolae Ceauşescu.

4. The Saudis did not discount what happened. Stories became widespread of people cast in Saudi dungeons for having tapes of Yemen's parliament. See for instance *al-Jazirat al-arabiyyah*, 29, 1993.

5. Paul Dresch, 'A Daily Plebiscite: Nation and State in Yemen', *Revue du monde musulman et de la méditerannée* 67 (1993/1), pp. 67–77; *al-Qabaliyyah wa-l-dimuqratiyyah*, trans. 'Alawi al-Saqqaf from lecture of September 30, 1992 (San'a', al-Markaz al-faransi li-l-dirasat al-yamaniyyah, 1994). English text in *Chroniques yéménites* vol. 2, 1994.

   The decay of popular enthusiasm can be followed by talking to people about local elections and local cooperatives (*ta'awuniyyat*). In 1980 the latter were perhaps the most dynamic local development force in the whole area; by 1990, having largely been centralized, they were a topic for depressing cynicism.

6. At the start of the 1980s 'Ali 'Abdullah Salih showed a remarkable ability to reconcile people who had once been his opponents, drawing them into the government system. With neighbors and relatives so entrenched, this would not now be easy to do.

   A line comes to mind which was used of Imam al-Mahdi al-'Abbas in the nineteenth century: *wa-la-hu haybah shadidah fi qulub khawassi-hi* (He struck dread in the hearts of his own favourites), Muhammad 'Ali al-Shawkani, *al-Badr al-tali'* (Beirut, Dar al-ma'rifah, n.d.), photo-reprint of first edition 1348 AH, vol. 1, p. 311. When that control was lost, as it seems to have been recently, Yemen's affairs decayed rapidly.

7. In the late 1970s and early 1980s tribal areas, beyond effective control from San'a', had a frightening reputation among foreigners in the capital. In fact, if one behaved oneself, they were perfectly safe: one was in far less danger there than in most parts of London. By the early 1990s this was not always true.

8. 'Ali Salim al-Bid's televised speech of September 25, 1992 made an enormous impression in the North. Some of 'Ali 'Abdullah Salih's speeches were well received in the South. But rhetoric on both sides, for four whole years, usually veered from implausible declarations of unanimity to scurrilous insults without ever pausing at public honesty.

9. One of the points agreed between the 'Alis was that the elections be postponed. Shaykh 'Abdullah of Hashid, two days before this, gave an interview in which he stressed how important it was that elections be held on schedule (*Yemen Times* 2:46, November 11, 1992). Not for the first

time, and not for the last, communications between the Shaykh and the president seemed less than perfect. One had the same impression over troubles with the 'Afghans' in Abyan in early 1993: see *al-Hayat* (London), January 3, 4 and 8, 1993.
10. The maneuvering that immediately preceded the war is summarized in *al-Watan al-'arabi* (Paris) 897, May 13, 1994. See also *al-Wasat* (London) 119, May 9, 1994.
11. That certain commanders of the Northern army thought in uncompromising terms is no surprise. Presumably the technocrats thought the political crisis had to be resolved quickly or the country would flounder—and then took too seriously what the generals promised.
12. *Al-Hayat*, March 4 and 11, 1994. The attempt to resolve the dispute between the two 'Alis went on for months, but a crux was the selection of Mujahid Abu Shawarib, Yahya al-Mutawakkil and Haytham Qasim Tahir to arrange security for a meeting between the president and vice-president. When that fell through, so did everything.

 Sinan Abu Lahum goes back to the very founding of the Republic in the North. If not quite in the Washington–Jefferson class as a founding father, he is certainly at the Hamilton–Madison level. Hence the power of his statement that if Yemen were divided he would not come back.
13. For an account of tribalism in North Yemen, see Paul Dresch, *Tribes, Government, and History in Yemen* (Oxford, Clarendon Press, 1989 and paperback 1993). In the South tribalism was ruthlessly suppressed for a quarter century. For which tribe is which, see Hamzah 'Ali Luqman, *Tarikh al-qaba'il al-yamaniyyah* (San'a', Dar al-Kalimah, 1985).
14. A great deal of socialist rhetoric is oddly colonialist, depicting tribes as remnants of another age. Western newspapers sometimes accept such imagery without a glimmer of thought. See e.g. *The Times* (London), May 9, 1994 and the *Guardian* (London), June 6, 1994.
15. The Tariq al-Fadli incident in Abyan (see *al-Hayat*, January 8, 1993) was a case in point. All that the tribes did was provide local mediation. In the years after unity there were a number of tribal meetings elsewhere in the South (see e.g. *al-Nahdah*, September 14, 1992), all of which proclaimed local truces but none of which declared a party allegiance.
16. On 'Awlaqi unwillingness to become involved, see *Le Monde* (Paris), May 25, 1994 and *The Sunday Times* (London), May 29, 1994. For some wishful thinking about tribes, see *al-Sharq al-awsat* (London), May 15, 1994, which also floats the old idea of dividing Yemen into minor statelets.
17. I disagree here with Charles Dunbar, 'The Unification of Yemen: Process, Politics, and Prospects', *Middle East Journal* 46:3 (Summer 1992), pp. 456–76.
18. It is said that, many months before the fighting, hard words passed between King Fahd and the Shaykh on this score.

Notes

During the fighting some play was made with television pictures of the Shaykh sitting next to the King, and other politicians from Yemen sitting much further off.

19. A parallel might be drawn with the Conservative Party in Britain, which contains some quite extreme right-wing nationalists—but to see the Conservative Party as simply a party of the far right would be to misunderstand British politics.
20. The details of Islamist politics are beyond the scope of this chapter. The different tiny groupings and their attachments to Saudi rulers, Saudi merchant families, Sudan, Brothers in Egypt, Brothers in West Germany and groups in Pakistan are a vast subject. In brief, the extremists are few in number and most people in the YRG are not extremists—indeed, much of the grouping's rhetoric is indistinguishable from that of the GPC. Egyptian visions of Yemen as potentially a 'new Sudan' are inaccurate if not downright mischievous.
21. See e.g. *al-Sharq al-awsat*, July 11, 1994. A certain Islamist style has spread since the fighting (ladies' hairdressers in San'a' have been closed, for instance). But Tariq al-Fadli, who of all the Islamists most deserved some reward for his military efforts, emerged only as police chief of Zinjibar—hardly a key post.
22. *Al-Watan al-'arabi* 897, May 13, 1994. The disagreement referred to in note 18 above is said to have involved suggesting (perhaps not very seriously) that funds would be diverted to 'Abd al-Majid al-Zindani.

There have long been links between fundamentalists and Hashidi tank-corps officers, but these are fundamentalists over whom the Shaykh perhaps has little influence. The games being played by different constituencies within the country need not detain us.
23. Such terms were used in private long before they were taken up in YSP propaganda.
24. 'Ali 'Abdullah Salih's mother ('Ali Maqsa's sister, I believe) was widowed fairly early in life and married the brother of her deceased husband. For a list of who's who, see *al-Watan al-'arabi* 897, 13 May 1994 and *al-Majallah* (London), 28 May 1994. For the position of other notables after the war, see the coverage in *al-Wasat* 131, August 1, 1994.
25. Some Western papers took this up (e.g. *The Independent* (London), May 24, 1994), rather misunderstanding the issue.
26. The term *'ashirah* has often been used in this polemical sense by people from the Southern governorates. See e.g. 'Abduh Husayn Adhal, *al-Istiqlal al-da'i* (Cairo, Dar al-'ahd, 1993). One also finds the term *qabaliyyah* used in this context by Sinan Abu Lahum (*al-Hayat*, March 11, 1994). Oddly, this might remind us that Shaykh Sinan, although much respected by tribesmen, built his own political career on a non-tribal base.
27. Again I have to differ with Charles Dunbar here ('Unification of

Yemen . . .', p. 467). The involvement of tribes with the state apparatus and the pre-unity enthusiasm of some tribes for the South was well established. See Paul Dresch, 'Tribal Relations and Political History in Upper Yemen', in B. R. Pridham (ed.), *Contemporary Yemen: Politics and Historical Background* (London, Croom Helm, 1984).
28. The incident was pounced on, from different angles, by *22 May* and *al-Tashih* (both on November 18, 1992).
29. Dresch, *Tribes, Government, and History* . . ., pp. 362–72.
30. For an account of the Bakil Council by one of those involved, see *al-Hayat*, January 7, 1994. The first big meeting was held in Anis on January 13.

    I note in passing that Muhammad Abu Lahum goes as far as I would myself, in saying that the fighting in Yemen was really not a civil war—in the North, at least, the population did not join in (*al-Hayat*, May 15, 1994).
31. Sadly, documentary evidence in private hands supports this contention.
32. A *tahjir* places a shaykh under the formal protection of those who recognize him. Shaykh 'Abdullah, one should note, is *muhajjar* not only from Hashid but from many Bakil tribes also.
33. I understand from recent conversations (Abu Dhabi, 1994) that this was viewed by diplomats as merely a Saudi ploy.
34. A vast number of letters in possession of the conference leadership express allegiance and hope for support. Some of them remind one of letters in British records from Aden in the early 1960s, when certain 'royalists' from the North made extraordinary claims about the size of 'their' tribe and in fact had a following of only a handful of cousins.
35. Obviously, different people may have aims of their own. But many of the *Talahum* people stressed repeatedly that they wished to have Shaykh 'Abdullah take part in peace-making; indeed, some wished he would take charge of the process. I see no reason to doubt their sincerity.
36. *Al-Sharq al-awsat*, January 20, 1993.
37. 'Abdullah Daris, for instance, was never a member of the National Cohesion Conference. He was, however, widely trusted and therefore asked to hold such things as truce documents.
38. Politics is a field where one often has two possible interpretations: either the principals are extremely cunning or they have it wrong. After almost two decades watching politics in Yemen (admittedly from the viewpoint of ordinary tribesmen, not the viewpoint of 'those who loose and bind'), I am convinced that neighboring governments understand the place very poorly. Perhaps the events of 1994 will convince other states in the peninsula that this is so.
39. The idea of the Saba' Conference seems first to have cohered when shaykhs from al-Qayifah and al-Bayda' came to the National Cohesion Conference *maqarr* (headquarters) in San'a', and then to meetings hosted in Arhab. Before this, Khawlan al-Tiyal had been involved in conflicts

with, and conflicts among, the tribes to their south and east. Now they formed the link between such tribes and Bakil tribes further north among whom the National Cohesion Conference had enjoyed success.

40. One of the organizers was telephoned from San‘a’ and told to return, because the meeting would only provoke 'tribal disorder'. Diplomatically, and with a nice touch of irony, he replied that he could not return because 'tribal disorder' meant the roads were not passable.

41. Some concern was expressed that Shaykh Muhammad's connections might prejudice his judgement. Plainly he set those worries to rest. The discussions were a clear example of the point made in note 33 above: if one acts as people wish, then broader political connections are no obstacle; if one acts against people's wishes, however, not all the connections and funding in the world will produce results.

42. Muhammad Naji al-Ghadir (Khawlan al-Tiyal), Muhsin ‘Ali Mu‘ayli (‘Abidah), ‘Ali al-Qibli Nimran (Murad), Muhsin Abu Nashtan (Arhab), ‘Ali Muhammad al-‘Ukaymi (Dhu Husayn), Sayf Ahmad al-Qibli (Murad), ‘Abd al-Hamid al-Qawsi (al-Hada), Sharif Husayn ‘Ali al-Dumayn (Jawf Ashraf), Ahmad al-Basha Zaba‘ (Nihm), ‘Abdullah al-Maqdashi (‘Ans) and Husayn Ahmad al-Rasas (of a famous *qadi* family).

43. Some of the organizers were angered by continued press references to the meeting as being 'anti-Hashid'. That is not what they were saying, nor had they ever said such a thing.

44. In the last few months before the fighting there were many such meetings in different areas. Some were purely local initiatives, others derived from the larger conferences; the aims of all of them seem to have been broadly similar.

45. Soon after the fighting a member of the government, in private conversation, denounced an organizer of the United Bakil Conference as a 'Saudi agent'. One trusts this was merely the result of tiredness.

    ‘Abd al-Majid al-Zindani takes a similar view, that any meeting not organized by himself must be factionalism sown by his enemies, in his case the socialists (see *al-Majallah* 753, July 23, 1994, p. 22). Such imaginings bode ill for Yemen.

46. Some Western accounts were bizarre: e.g. 'as a Northern army encircles Aden and tribal leaders rouse their formidable militias to join the conflict' (*The Sunday Times*, May 8, 1994). Who? Where? Not for the first time, one had the impression of journalists, sitting in front of their word-processors, simply guessing.

47. For an eloquent defence of tribal morals, in the abstract, see *al-Sahwah*, 340, November 26, 1992. In practice, an attempt was made by Shaykh ‘Abdullah to organize a conference of tribes in February–March 1994: the results were reportedly disappointing.

Chapter 3
1. Personal communication from a senior Yemeni official.
2. Sheila Carapico, 'From Ballot Box to Battlefield: The War of the Two 'Alis', *Middle East Report* 25:1 (no. 190, September–October 1994), p. 27.
3. Personal communication from a knowledgeable Yemeni observer.
4. A leading Southern politician asserted to the writer in August 1994 that President Salih was said to be prepared to concede this constitutional point to the YRG in return for unspecified YRG concessions in other areas.
5. A San'a' University professor told the writer that, because of YRG harassment, the former dean of the Political Science Department had already left the country and that he himself was considering a similar move.
6. A case of a Southerner rallying to the North when the creation of the Democratic Republic of Yemen was announced was that of Fadhl Muhsin 'Abdullah. Fadhl Muhsin, a member of the Political Bureau of the Yemeni Socialist Party, had been minister of fisheries in the government in San'a' before the civil war. Prior to the outbreak of the fighting, he went to the South, first to Aden and then to his home region, and his son was killed fighting for the South. However, when the establishment of the new Republic was announced, he returned to San'a' and announced that he was joining the Northern cause. He was reinstated in the government and was the cause of the walk-out of the YRG members of the cabinet when it met in Aden on July 14, 1994.
7. Personal communication to the writer in August 1994 from a leading Southern politician.
8. US Arms Control and Disarmament Agency, *World Military Expenditures and Arms Transfers 1991–1992* (Washington DC, 1994), pp. 35–46. In 1991, in terms of military expenditure as a percentage of GNP, Yemen ranked tenth among 142 countries surveyed with a figure of 14.4% (p. 39).

Chapter 4
1. For an early analysis of Yemeni unification, see Charles Dunbar, 'The Unification of Yemen: Process, Politics, and Prospects', *Middle East Journal* 46:3 (Summer 1992), pp. 456–76. For the present author's thinking on Yemeni politics, see Robert D. Burrowes, *The Yemen Arab Republic: The Politics of Development 1962–1986* (Boulder, CO, Westview Press, 1987); 'Oil Strike and Leadership Crisis in South Yemen: 1986 and Beyond', *Middle East Journal* 43:3 (Summer 1989), pp. 437–54; and 'The Yemen Arab Republic's Legacy and Yemeni Unification', *Arab Studies Quarterly* 14:4 (Fall 1992), pp. 41–68. Also available from the author is 'The Republic of Yemen: A Case of Political Unification in Process, 1989–1992', a paper prepared for the Conference on Arab Integration, Georgetown University, April 1992.

Notes

2. It seems that the Kuwaitis were motivated primarily by a strong desire to punish Yemen for its stand during the Gulf crisis and war in 1990–91; by contrast, the Saudis, although attributed by others with the same motive, seem to have been motivated mostly by the desire to destroy the populous, unified, democratizing Yemen that they deeply feared and distrusted.

    Throughout most of the civil war, the immediate cessation of fighting would probably have led to the de facto re-division of Yemen, the obvious goal of the Southern forces and most of their supporters abroad. Ironically, in its ambiguity of motive and likely effect, the stand taken by most of the GCC states—immediate cessation of hostilities, disengagement of forces and international truce supervision—is reminiscent of Yemen's call for an Arab diplomatic-political solution to the Gulf crisis of 1990–91. At that time, it was argued by most observers that the position taken by Yemen would have resulted in the permanent absorption of Kuwait by Iraq.

3. Opponents of North Yemen referred to President Salih as a 'little Saddam', but one controlled by Islamic fundamentalists in a way more analogous to President Bashir in Sudan than to Saddam Hussein in Iraq; others referred to the regime as 'Ahmar's gang', a reference to Shaykh 'Abdullah bin Husayn al-Ahmar, head of the Hashid tribal confederation and leader of the Yemeni Reform Grouping (YRG or Islah). Not to be outdone by their opponents, supporters of North Yemen called the Southern regime the 'Republic of Makallah' and noted that it was led in Aden by 'Abd al-Rahman al-Jifri, a Saudi citizen.

4. Had the Southern effort succeeded, the old assumption of virtual equality between the two Yemens would probably have been inapplicable to the new situation. The reborn South Yemen would probably have been another mini-state of disparate parts, a small population, modest oil resources, and modest development potential—i.e. quite like Oman.

5. Saudi fears of and ambivalence towards Yemen are legendary. 'Abdul 'Aziz ibn Saud, the founder of the Kingdom of Saudi Arabia, is said to have told his sons on his deathbed that 'the good or evil for us will come from Yemen'. King Faysal and Prince Sultan, among others, seem to have taken this to heart.

6. For Saudi-Yemeni relations through the mid-1980s, see F. Gregory Gause III, *Saudi-Yemeni Relations: Domestic Structures and Foreign Influences* (New York, Columbia University Press, 1990). For a more current treatment of the subject, see Mark Katz, 'Yemeni Unity and Saudi Security', *Middle East Policy* 1:1 (1992), pp. 117–35.

7. An occurrence during a conference in San'a' in September 1992 on 'Yemen and the New World Order' illustrates my point. I was naive enough to suggest in a public address that Saudi Arabia's need for people and Yemen's need for oil-bearing land provided the basis for a people-for-land deal in which the Yemenis would give up their claim to the populous 'Northern

111

provinces' in exchange for a generous Saudi offer regarding the disputed territory in the east and north of the Hadramawt, an area where oil reserves were suspected. After I was severely criticized by several Yemeni speakers for suggesting that Yemen should trade away any of its 'sacred homeland', an apologetic Yemeni diplomat took me aside and told me that the foreign ministry was currently exploring a trade-off of this sort. But that was in 1992, not 1994.
8. There is an Indian saying that goes something like the following: When the elephants fight, the blades of grass are likely to get broken.
9. For studies of Saudi Arabia and its external relations, see William Quandt, *Saudi Arabia in the 1980s: Foreign Policy, Security and Oil* (Washington DC, The Brookings Institution, 1981); and Nadav Safran, *Saudi Arabia: The Ceaseless Quest for Security* (Cambridge, MA, Harvard University Press, 1985). For a current treatment of this subject, see Mordechai Abir, *Saudi Arabia: Government, Society and the Gulf Crisis* (New York, Routledge, 1993).
10. For these developments in the early 1990s, see Abir, *Saudi Arabia*...
11. The public disclosure in August 1994 that Saudi Arabia had apparently bought a whole squadron of Russian MiG-29s, complete with Russian pilots, for the secessionists during the civil war certainly did not help matters.
12. The isolation and non-isolation scenarios and their implications were developed at the ECSSR symposium in the paper by Mark Katz (see Chapter 5), and are relevant to the point being made here.
13. During a discussion session at the ECSSR symposium, Michael Hudson raised the possibility of GCC membership or something like NATO's new 'partnership for peace' status for Yemen. I suggested that Yemen could provide the GCC with the population base necessary to muster an army of credible size. Neither idea will be feasible in the foreseeable future.

Chapter 5
1. The first intra-Yemeni conflict was the 1962–70 North Yemeni civil war between royalists and republicans. The second was the 1964–67 war for independence in South Yemen, which was just as much a conflict between two rival 'national liberation movements' (the Marxist National Liberation Front and the Nasserist Front for the Liberation of South Yemen) as it was a fight against the British. The third was the 1972 border war between the North and the South. The fourth was the 1979 border war between the North and the South. The fifth was the 1979–82 South Yemeni-backed National Democratic Front insurgency against North Yemen. The sixth was the brief but vicious 1986 civil war in South Yemen between rival factions of the ruling Yemeni Socialist Party (YSP).
2. Officials in San'a' believe that Saudi Arabia was aiding the South even

before the conflict. The text of a purportedly secret memo from the Yemeni foreign ministry detailing Saudi-YSP collaboration was published before the war in *al-Muharrir* (Paris), April 25, 1994, p. 7.

How true the charges are is uncertain, but San'a' undoubtedly believed them.
3. 'Yemen: The End?', *The Economist* (London), July 9, 1994, p. 43.
4. International Institute for Strategic Studies, *The Military Balance 1993-1994* (London, Brassey's, 1993), p. 133.
5. *The Economist* reported that the South acquired MiG-29s 'from old Warsaw Pact stockpiles', but does not state from which particular country. It is doubtful that any country possessing such aircraft would have provided them for free; someone had to buy them. Since the South was not in a position to do so, US and Yemeni sources speculate that the Saudis and/or other GCC states must have done so for them. See 'Yemen: The End?', p. 43.
6. 'Yemen Says Southern Remnants Have Fled to Other Countries', *Washington Post*, July 11, 1994.

The Saudi interior minister, Prince Nayif, denied this: Saudi Arabian Television Network (Riyadh), July 13, 1994.
7. For a fuller discussion of the issues dividing Saudi Arabia and Yemen before the 1994 civil war, see Mark N. Katz, 'Yemeni Unity and Saudi Security', *Middle East Policy* 1:1 (1992), pp. 117-35.
8. 'Yemen: The End?', p.43.
9. 'Northern Yemeni Troops Take Portions of Southern Port', *Washington Post*, July 7, 1994.
10. At the end of the conflict, the Kuwaiti information minister, Shaykh Sa'ud Nasir Al Sabah, stated, "Ali 'Abdullah Salih is an ally of Saddam Hussein and we have no feeling of liking for him.' Commenting on the defeat of the South, he said, 'What happened in Yemen was not acceptable and we have not yet seen the end of it. The bloodshed will continue': *Reuter* (Cairo), July 13, 1994.
11. 'Yemen Says Southern Remnants Have Fled . . .'
12. Conversations with Qatari diplomats in Washington and Doha, July 1994.
13. The Southern foreign minister, 'Abdallah al-Asnaj, claimed that twenty Jordanian military experts were 'seen at the San'a' air base': *MENA* (Cairo), June 10, 1994.
14. Al-Asnaj also claimed that Southern forces had captured seven Iraqi military experts who had been aiding the Northern forces. He claimed that 'the war machines of North Yemen are completely under the control of these experts': *ibid*.

While vociferously condemning the Southerners, the Iraqis hotly denied giving military assistance to the North. They claimed that the captured Iraqis were in fact 'teachers who were on contract in Yemen': see 'Isa

Isma'il al-'Abbadi, 'The Lies of the Separatists', *al-Thawrah* (Baghdad), July 3, 1994, p. 2.

15. When it came to specifics, however, this statement only mentioned 'a team of electrical and water engineers': *SUNA* (Khartoum), July 10, 1994.
16. San'a' publicly thanked Libya for sending a 'medical team' to San'a': *JANA* (Tripoli), July 11, 1994.
17. Haleh Vaziri, 'Iran and Saudi Arabia in the 1990s', *US-Iran Review* (April–May 1994), pp. 1 and 4–5.

    Iranian commentary, however, heavily criticized the GCC for even considering recognition of South Yemen. According to one broadcast, 'The GCC foreign ministers not only failed to take a step towards solving the crisis of civil war in Yemen but worked towards continuing it. Political experts believe that the stand does not reflect the policies of the GCC countries but rather the dangerous game that [Saudi] Arabia is pursuing under cover of the GCC': *Voice of the Islamic Republic of Iran* (Tehran), June 6, 1994.
18. While expressing support for the cause of Yemeni unity, Tehran vigorously denied a story in *Le Point* (Paris), that Iran was supplying weapons to San'a': Yemeni Republic Radio Network (San'a'), June 14, 1994.
19. See, for example, National Democratic Institute for International Affairs, *Promoting Participation in Yemen's 1993 Elections* (Washington DC, NDIIA, 1994).
20. For a general statement on the US position on the Yemeni civil war, see the 'Opening Statement' of Robert H. Pelletreau, assistant secretary of state for Near Eastern affairs, before the House Subcommittee on Europe and the Middle East, 14 June 1994, pp. 4–5.
21. Oman and the UAE (as well as Djibouti) reportedly agreed to return to San'a' the aircraft and ships which Southern forces had used to flee to their territory: *MENA* (Cairo), July 16, 1994.

    The Omani information minister, 'Abd al-'Aziz al-Rawwas, visited San'a' and met with President Salih on July 11. He reportedly told him that al-Bid, who had fled to Oman, had 'renounced politics'. An exiled Southern source in Jiddah, though, denied that al-Bid had made any such promise: *AFP* (Paris), July 18, 1994.
22. For recent reports on Saudi opposition activities, see Caryle Murphy, 'Exiled Saudi Dissidents Launch Media Campaign', *Washington Post*, June 1, 1994; 'Saudi Stability', *Washington Post*, June 23, 1994; Steve Coll, 'Saudi Defections Pressure West to Balance Policy toward Riyadh', *Washington Post*, July 2, 1994; and John Mintz, 'Official's Asylum Request Could Complicate Saudi-US Diplomacy', *Washington Post*, July 8, 1994.
23. 'Yemen Says Southern Remnants Have Fled . . .'.

Notes

Conclusion
1. The Economist Intelligence Unit, *Yemen Country Profile 1994–95* (London, The Economist Group, 1994), p. 48.
2. *Ibid.*, pp. 41 and 44.
3. Andrew Rathmell, 'Civil War in Yemen', *The World in Conflict: Jane's Intelligence Review Yearbook* (London, Jane's Information Group, 1994), p. 88.
4. Quoted in US Congress, Congressional Research Service, *Yemen: Civil Strife*, by Alfred Prados, Issue Brief (July 15, 1994), p. 10.

Select Bibliography

Abir, Mordechai. *Saudi Arabia: Government, Society and the Gulf Crisis*, New York, Routledge, 1993.

Adhal,'Abduh Husayn. *Al-Istiqlal al-da'i'*, Cairo, Dar al-'ahd, 1993.

Burrowes, Robert D. *The Yemen Arab Republic: The Politics of Development, 1962-1986*, Boulder, CO, Westview Press, 1987.

——*The Republic of Yemen: An Historical Dictionary*, forthcoming.

——*The Republic of Yemen: Oil and Unification*, forthcoming.

——'Oil Strike and Leadership Crisis in South Yemen: 1986 and Beyond', *Middle East Journal* 43:3 (Summer 1989), pp. 437-54.

——'Prelude to Unification: The Yemen Arab Republic, 1962-90', *International Journal of Middle East Studies* 23:4 (November 1991), pp. 483-506.

——'The Republic of Yemen: A Case of Political Unification in Process, 1989-1992', paper prepared for the Conference on Arab Integration, Georgetown University, April 1992.

——'The Yemen Arab Republic's Legacy and Yemeni Unification', *Arab Studies Quarterly* 14:4 (Fall 1992), pp. 41-68.

Carapico, Sheila. 'Elections and Mass Politics in Yemen', *Middle East Report* 23:6 (no. 185, November-December 1993), pp. 2-6.

——'From Ballot Box to Battlefield: The War of the Two 'Alis', *Middle East Report* 25:1 (no. 190, September-October 1994), p. 27.

Democratic Republic of Yemen, Office of the Council of Ministers, 'Verbal Note', *al-Makallah*, June 12, 1994.

Detalle, Renaud, 'The Yemeni Elections Up Close', *Middle East Report* 23:6 (no. 185, November-December 1993), pp. 8-12.

Deutsch, Karl, et al. *Political Community and the North Atlantic Area*, Princeton NJ, Princeton University Press, 1957, pp. 5-9.

Dresch, Paul K. *Tribes, Government and History in Yemen*, Oxford, Clarendon Press, 1989.

——'Tribal Relations and Political History in Upper Yemen', in B. R. Pridham (ed.), *Contemporary Yemen: Politics and Historical Background*, London, Croom Helm, 1984.

Select Bibliography

——'A Daily Plebiscite: Nation and State in Yemen', *Revue du monde musulman et de la méditerannée* 67 (1993/1), pp. 67–77.

Dunbar, Charles. 'The Unification of Yemen: Process, Politics, and Prospects', *Middle East Journal* 46:3 (Summer 1992), pp. 456–76.

Economist Intelligence Unit, The. *Yemen Country Profile 1994–95*, London, The Economist Group, 1994, p. 48.

Gause III, F. Gregory. *Saudi-Yemeni Relations: Domestic Structures and Foreign Influences*, New York, Columbia University Press, 1990.

Hudson, Michael C. *Arab Politics: The Search for Legitimacy*, Yale University Press, 1977.

——*The Precarious Republic: Political Modernization in Lebanon*, Boulder, CO, Westview Press, 1985.

—— (ed.). *The Palestinians: New Directions*, Georgetown University (CCAS), 1990.

——'After the Gulf War: Prospects for Democratization in the Arab World', *Middle East Journal* 45:3 (Summer 1991), pp. 407–26.

International Institute for Strategic Studies, *The Military Balance 1993–1994*, London, Brassey's, 1993, p. 133.

Katz, Mark N. *Russia and Arabia: Soviet Foreign Policy Toward the Arabian Peninsula*, Baltimore, MD, Johns Hopkins Press, 1986.

——'Yemeni Unity and Saudi Security', *Middle East Policy* 1:1 (1992), pp. 117–35.

Luqman, Hamzah 'Ali. *Tarikh al-qaba'il al-yamaniyyah*, San'a', Dar al-Kalimah, 1985.

Middle East Watch, 'Yemen: Steps toward Civil Society', *Middle East Watch* 4:10 (November 1992).

Myles, John, 'Yemen's Growing Pains', *Middle East International* no. 438 (November 20, 1992).

National Democratic Institute for International Affairs, *Promoting Participation in Yemen's 1993 Elections*, Washington DC, NDIIA, 1994.

Prados, Alfred. *Yemen: Civil Strife*, US Congress, Congressional Research Service, Issue Brief (July 15, 1994), p. 10.

Pridham, B. R. (ed.). *Contemporary Yemen: Politics and Historical Background*, London, Croom Helm, 1984.

——(ed.). *Economy, Society and Culture in Contemporary Yemen*, London, Croom Helm, 1985.

Quandt, William. *Saudi Arabia in the 1980s: Foreign Policy, Security and Oil*, Washington DC, The Brookings Institution, 1981.

Select Bibliography

Rondot, Pierre. *Les Institutions Politiques du Liban*, no pub., Paris, 1947.

Safran, Nadav. *Saudi Arabia: The Ceaseless Quest for Security*, Cambridge, MA, Harvard University Press, 1985.

US Arms Control and Disarmament Agency, *World Military Expenditures and Arms Transfers 1991–1992*, Washington DC, 1994, pp. 35–46.

Vaziri, Haleh. 'Iran and Saudi Arabia in the 1990s', *US-Iran Review* (April–May 1994), pp. 1 and 4–5.

Warburton, David, 'The War in Yemen', unpublished paper, San'a', June 1994.

Watkins, Eric. 'Opening the Way', *Middle East International* no. 412, November 8, 1991.

——'Yemen's Riots Prompt Talk of Reform', *Middle East International* no. 444, February 19, 1993, p. 18.

Watkins, Eric, and Patrick Makin. 'Yemen's Crisis Threatens the Country's Unity', *Middle East International* no. 463, November 19, 1993.

Whittaker, Brian, 'Up to the Brink', *Middle East International* no. 461, October 22, 1993.

Index

'Abidah 44, 45, 47
Abu Dhabi 12, 76
Abu Lahum, Sinan 36, 62
Abu Nashtan, Muhsin 48
Abu Ra's, Hamud 47
Abu Shawarib, Mujahid 37, 43, 60, 64
Aden 22, 24, 25, 27, 28, 30, 34, 64, 65, 73, 98
Afghanistan; Afghans 39, 64
al-Ahmar, Shaykh 'Abdullah bin Husayn 29, 39–41, 45, 49, 55, 62, 64, 65, 91; see also Bayt al-Ahmar
'A'id, Muhammad 50
al-Ajda', Ghalib 45
Algeria 14, 89
Algiers 66
al-'Amalisah 48
America 32, 81, 87; see also United States; Washington
Amman 26
Al 'Ammar 48
'Amran 36, 41
'Amran Conference (1963) 45
Anis 45
'Ans 44
Arab Gulf states 16, 71–80 passim, 92, 95
Arabian peninsula 12, 15–17, 23, 71–80 passim, 89, 95
Arhab 48
'Asir 74, 82, 96
al-'Atif 48
al-'Attas, Haydar Abu Bakr 22, 24, 25
Austro-Hungarian empire 20–21
al-'Awadhil 37
'Awlaq 38

Baghdad 86; see also Iraq
Bahrain 84
Bakil 36, 37, 40, 41, 43, 45, 46, 48, 50, 52–55, 60, 62, 63
Bakil Conference see United Bakil Conference
Bakil Council 45
Bani Nawf 47
Bani Suraym 41, 48
Barat 48, 49, 50
al-Bayda' 46, 53
Bayhan 45
Bayt al-Ahmar 39, 42, 48; see also al-Ahmar, Shaykh 'Abdullah bin Husayn
Bayt Daris 43
Bayt Dhayban 48
Bayt Haydar 48
al-Bid, Vice-President 'Ali Salim 22, 25, 26, 27, 30, 31, 33, 35, 36, 38, 49, 57, 65, 85, 96
bin Jallal, 'Ali Hasan 44
bin Mu'ayli, Muhsin 'Ali 44

Cairo 66
Canada 87
Carapico, Sheila 31
China 63, 89
Cold War 11, 13, 16, 72, 78, 81, 86, 87, 92, 95, 96, 99

Index

Conference of Yemeni Tribes (previously Saba' Conference) 53
Council of Ministers 24

Dahm 47
Damascus 69
Daris, 'Abdullah 43, 47
'Democratic Republic of Yemen' 26, 67
Deutsch, Karl 20, 32
al-Dhahab, Nasir 45
Dhamar 25, 36
Dhu Husayn 47, 50
Dhu Muhammad 41, 43, 47, 48, 50, 63
Document of Concern and Reconciliation 26
al-Dumaynah 48

Eastern bloc 33; Eastern Europe 88
Egypt; Egyptians 14, 27, 42, 84, 89
Exxon 87

Fahd, King 40, 49, 92, 99
France 89

GCC *see* Gulf Cooperation Council
General People's Congress (GPC) 13, 21, 22, 24, 27–30 *passim*, 32, 34, 35, 44, 50, 65, 91
Geneva 27
Germany, East 34
Germany, West 34
al-Ghadir, Muhammad Naji 51, 52
al-Ghadir, Naji bin 'Ali 46
al-Ghashmi, Ahmad 41, 42
Gore, Vice-President Al 27
GPC *see* General People's Congress

Gulf Cooperation Council (GCC) 16, 17, 27, 71, 75–80 *passim*, 81, 85, 87–90 *passim*, 92, 93, 95, 98, 99, 100
Gulf crisis (1990–91) 24, 26, 46, 66, 73–79 *passim*, 97; *see also* Gulf war
Gulf states *see* Arab Gulf states
Gulf war (1990–91) 15, 16, 25, 35, 57, 60, 61, 74, 83, 85, 90, 92, 95, 97; *see also* Gulf crisis

al-Hada 44, 45
Haddah 44
Hadramawt 28, 38, 58, 66, 73, 74
Hajjah Conference 54
Al Hamad 47
Hamdan 41
al-Hamdi, Ibrahim 41, 45
Hantash, 'Ali bin Muhammad 47
Hapsburg 20
Harashah 47
al-Harith 45
Hashid 29, 30, 37, 39–43 *passim*, 45, 48, 49, 52, 55, 60, 62, 63, 64, 91
Hashid Solidarity Conference 41
al-Hayyal, Salih bin 'Ali 46
al-Hazm 43
Hizb al-Haqq 49
Hudaydah 36
Hunt Oil Co. 87
Hussein, President Saddam 57, 83, 84

al-Ibrahimi, al-Akhdar 26
International Institute for Strategic Studies 82
Iran; Iranians 17, 73, 79, 86, 89, 92, 98; *see also* Tehran
Iraq; Iraqis 17, 24, 25, 46, 61, 73, 79, 83, 85–86, 89, 90, 92, 98
Islah 13, 14, 21, 29, 30, 39, 64, 86,

Index

97; *see also* Yemeni Reform Grouping
'Iyal Yazid 43

Jawf 43, 45, 46
al-Jifri, 'Abd al-Rahman 36
Jizan 74, 96
Jordan 85

Khamir Conference (1965) 45
Kharif 37, 41
Khawlan 34, 46–47, 50, 63
Khawlan al-Tiyal 45–47
Khiyar 48
Korea, North 88
Kuwait; Kuwaitis 24, 26, 46, 75, 76, 78, 83–88 *passim*, 92, 97

Lebanon 19, 27
Libya 86

Madhhij 37, 41, 45, 54, 55
al-Mahashimah 47
al-Maranat 48
Ma'rib 43, 45, 63
Moscow 87; *see also* Russia; Union of Soviet Socialist Republics
Muhammad, 'Ali Nasir 66
Murad 44, 45, 51
Muslim Brotherhood 22

Najran 74, 96
Nasiris 43
National Cohesion Conference (1991) 47–51 *passim*, 53
National Construction and Reform Programme 24
National Dialogue Committee 26, 28, 36
National Endowment for Democracy [United States] 87
Nihm 36, 43, 44, 62
Nimran, 'Ali al-Qibli 52

Norway 21
Nu'man, Dr. Yasin Sa'id 23, 25

Occidental 87
Oman; Omanis 37, 73, 75, 77, 78, 84, 85, 88, 97

Pact of Solidarity (1990) 47
People's Democratic Republic of Yemen (PDRY)/South Yemen *passim*; *see also* Aden
Presidential Council 27, 55, 64, 65, 83

Qadhdhafi, Colonel Muammar 86
Qahtan 55
Qatar 77, 85, 87, 88
al-Qayifah 45
Qays 48

Radfan 38
Raydah 48, 51
Riyadh 26, 39, 82–93 *passim*, 97, 98; *see also* Saudi Arabia
Rondot, Pierre 19
Russia 87, 89; *see also* Union of Soviet Socialist Republics

Saba' Conference (1992) (subsequently Conference of Yemeni Tribes) 50–53 *passim*
Sa'dah 47, 49, 63
Salih, President 'Ali 'Abdullah 14, 24–31, 35, 36, 39–42, 49, 57–64, 71, 73, 82–86, 88, 90, 91, 92, 96–100
Salih, 'Ali Muhsin 41
Salih, 'Ali Salih 'Abdullah 41
Salih, Muhammad 41
Salih, Salim 44
Al Salim 48
al-Sallam, 'Abd al-Wasi 25
San'a' 14, 20, 22, 23, 25–28, 30–32,

36, 39, 41, 43, 44, 48–50,
  57–59, 61–64, 66–70, 81–84,
  86–88, 90–92, 96–100
San'a' University 66
Sanhan 30, 34, 40–44 *passim*, 51,
  52, 63
Al Saud 39
Saudi Arabia; Saudis 14–16, 23,
  24, 26, 27, 30, 39, 40, 43, 45,
  46, 49, 51, 57, 63, 66, 69,
  71–80 *passim*, 82–93 *passim*,
  95–99 *passim*; *see also* Riyadh
Sayyah 34
Shabwah 12, 37
al-Shayif, Naji bin 'Abd al-'Aziz
  50, 63–64
al-Shayif, Naji Bajjash 50
Solidarity Conference of Yemeni
  Tribes (1990) 46, 49, 54
Somalia 85
Somaliland Republic 85
Soviet Union *see* Union of Soviet
  Socialist Republics
Sudan; Sudanese 73, 79, 86, 89, 92
Sufyan 48
Sultan, Prince 49
Summons to Truce (1990) 47
Sweden 21
Syria 84

Tahir, Haythan Qasim 25
Ta'if Treaty (1934) 74, 82, 96
Ta'izz 30
Ta'izz Conference 54
Tehran 66, 89; *see also* Iran
Thawabah, 'Abdullah Muhsin 47
Turkey 89

UAE *see* United Arab Emirates
'Umar, Jarallah 23
Union of Soviet Socialist
  Republics (USSR) 81, 82, 86,
  92; Soviet bloc 27; *see also*
  Moscow; Russia
United Arab Emirates (UAE)
  71–80 *passim*, 84, 88, 97
United Bakil Conference (1994)
  52, 53
United Nations (UN) 26, 85, 86,
  87, 89
United States (US) 21, 27, 34, 40,
  54, 78, 85, 86–87, 92; *see also*
  America; Washington
US Agency for International
  Development 87
al-'Usaymat 41

Wadi Dhannah 50
Washington 27, 86, 87, 91; *see also*
  America; United States
West; Western 16, 25, 31, 33, 34,
  43, 49, 54, 57, 67, 68, 81, 83,
  85, 87, 89, 90, 98

Yafi' 37, 38
al-Yemda 27
Yemen, North/Yemen Arab
  Republic (YAR) *passim*; *see
  also* San'a'
Yemen, South/People's
  Democratic Republic of
  Yemen (PDYR) *passim*; *see also*
  Aden
Yemeni Reform Grouping (YRG
  or Islah) 13, 14, 21, 39, 64–66,
  69, 86, 91–92; *see also* Islah
Yemeni Socialist Party (YSP) 13,
  21–32 *passim*, 34–37 *passim*, 41,
  44, 47–50 *passim*, 57, 61, 65, 69

Zaydis 49
al-Zindani, Shaykh 'Abd al-Majid
  29, 64, 86, 91